Praise for William J. Bennett

"William Bennett is a unique figure in American political life—a man with strong, *reasoned* convictions who speaks a language both clear and thoughtful. He almost alone talks seriously about the content of education, and his example proves that now a public figure has to be courageous indeed to praise the reading of good books."

—Allan Bloom, author of
The Closing of the American Mind

"William Bennett is the best thing that's happened to the Reagan administration. If, as we all hope, this country is saved from the educational disaster which has overtaken it, the first man we should thank is William Bennett."

—Walker Percy

"Whether writing about morality, teaching, or the skyrocketing costs of college tuition, Bill Bennett delights in proving that the Emperor has no clothes and that the conventional wisdom is not particularly wise. Anyone concerned with education in this country—from parents to college presidents—ought to take a good hard look at this collection of speeches."

—The Honorable Thomas Kean,
Governor of New Jersey

"Bill Bennett is that rare combination: a man of ideas who gets things done. His leadership and courage under fire have already started to put our educational system back on the road to excellence. There is no doubt that his continued leadership is critical to the future of the conservative movement in America."

—Congressman Jack Kemp

IMPROVING AMERICA'S SCHOOLS AND AFFIRMING THE COMMON CULTURE

Our

Children
and
Our Country

William J. Bennett

A TOUCHSTONE BOOK
Published by Simon & Schuster Inc.
NEW YORK   LONDON   TORONTO   SYDNEY   TOKYO

This book contains edited versions of speeches given by the former Secretary of Education in his official capacity. Neither Secretary Bennett nor the Department of Education will receive compensation for this book. However, a portion of proceeds from sales will be donated by Simon and Schuster to the Department of Education as a contribution toward the Department's annual School Recognition Program. The contents of these speeches are in the public domain. Editing copyright © 1988 Simon & Schuster Inc.

Touchstone
Simon & Schuster Building
Rockefeller Center
1230 Avenue of the Americas
New York, New York 10020

All rights reserved
including the right of reproduction
in whole or in part in any form.
First Touchstone Edition September, 1989
TOUCHSTONE and colophon are registered
trademarks of Simon & Schuster Inc.
Designed by Edith Fowler
Manufactured in the United States of America

10 9 8 7 6 5 4 3 2

10 9 8 7 6 5 4 3 2 1 Pbk.

Library of Congress Cataloging in Publication Data
Bennett, William John, date.
  Our children and our country : improving America's schools and affirming the common culture / William J. Bennett.
  p. cm.
    Includes index.
    1. Education—United States—Aims and objectives. 2. Public schools—United States. I. Title.
LA217.B44   1988
370.11'0973—dc 19   88–17498
ISBN 0-671-67062-X
ISBN 0-671-68735-2 Pbk.

To ELAYNE,
*who sent me out of my government office
and into America's classrooms, with love;
and*
To JOHN,
*whom we shall send, with love and hope,
into those same classrooms.*

Contents

Introduction

WHEN THE American people are asked what they want from our schools, they consistently put two tasks at the top of their list: first, teach our children how to speak, write, read, think, and count correctly; and second, help them to develop reliable standards of rights and wrong that will guide them through life.

These views have deep roots in America. At the time of our nation's founding, Thomas Jefferson listed the requirements for a sound education in the Report of the Commissioners for the University of Virginia. In this landmark statement on American education, Jefferson wrote of the importance of calculation and writing, and of reading, history, and geography. But he also emphasized the need "to instruct the mass of our citizens in these, their rights, interests, and duties, as men and citizens." Jefferson believed education should aim at the improvement of both one's "morals" and "faculties."

Jefferson's view has been the dominant view of the aims of American education for over two centuries, and remains the view of the American people today. Unfortunately, in recent decades, our schools fell away from the principles of our tradition.

In the 1960s and 1970s, we neglected and denied much of the best in American education. We simply stopped doing the right things. We allowed an assault on intellectual and moral standards.

Traditional education practices were discarded, expectations were lowered, and the curriculum was "dumbed-down." The "values clarification" movement, which asserted that education should not impart ethical standards and moral principles, gained currency.

The effects were damaging to our educational well-being. We saw an alarming drop in standardized test scores, and American students suffered in virtually all international comparisons. As educators chose to remain neutral on moral matters and to shun the development of character, we saw an increase in various pathologies among young people. Our children were too often the victims of adults' indulgences in educational and social foolishness. During the 1960s and 1970s, Americans nearly doubled spending in real terms on education—and we experienced the *worst* education decline in our history.

In reaction to this, the 1980s gave birth to a grass-roots movement for education reform that has generated a renewed commitment to excellence, character, and fundamentals. The American people are thus now engaged in the long struggle to rebuild an educational system worthy of our ideals. We are engaged in what Tom Wolfe has called a "great relearning." Much remains to be done, but we have reason for optimism, for much *is* being relearned.

The national debate on education is now focused on truly important matters: mastering the basics—math, history, science, and English; insisting on high standards and expectations; ensuring discipline in the classroom; conveying a grasp of our moral and political principles; and nurturing the character of the young. As a result, we have begun to see progress; we see real signs of educational renewal.

Of course, educational excellence depends on more than improvements in our curriculum, or higher test scores. In the end, a country must be judged by the quality of the citizens it produces. This means not just their skills and knowledge, but also their character, their virtue, and their interest in the common good. One of education's purposes is to animate and inform our public life, our civic life. A concern for education therefore reaches beyond issues like curricular reform and school governance, to matters such as the defense of our country and the nurture and protection of our children.

Our Children and Our Country comprises my thoughts on the state of American education and on the larger issues that any discussion of education necessarily raises. This volume includes twenty-four speeches I have delivered as Secretary of Education over the past three-and-one-half years. It is divided into seven sections, beginning with remarks about what works in education, about the fundamental principles of effective education. This section is followed by accounts of educators who are making it work. The third section addresses the central role that moral education must play in our schools. The promise and the shortcomings of higher education are the subject of the fourth section, while the fifth concerns the need for our students to achieve a greater understanding of our common culture—our common language, history, and traditions. The sixth section argues for the defense of Western political principles, and the seventh section concludes with a chapter on the prospects for education reform and my reflections on the legacy of the Reagan presidency.

The speeches have been edited and abridged, but what is presented here remains faithful to the original texts. I would like to thank those at the Department of Education and outside who helped on various aspects of the thinking, research, and editing of these speeches. Of course, the responsibility for the views expressed herein is mine alone. I am pleased that Simon and Schuster has decided to donate a portion of proceeds from sales from the book to the Department of Education as a contribution toward our annual School Recognition Program.

Education's best claim, according to William James, is that it teaches a person to value what deserves to be valued. Our common faith teaches us to cherish our country—its ideals and standards—and our children. For it is our children who will receive the promise of those ideals and standards, and upon whom will fall the task of defending them. As we proceed to meet our responsibilities to both our children and our country, I offer the following reflections as a contribution.

PART
ONE

WHAT
WORKS
IN
EDUCATION

ONE

The Three C's*

EDUCATORS IN AMERICA always have had three depend-
able, unfailing guides to elementary and secondary school curricula: the three R's—reading, writing, and arithmetic. But the
educational challenges we face today invite us to consider a new
trilogy of ideas. Not ideas that would replace the three R's; the
three R's will always be in season, every season. But now we must
also attend to the "three C's": content, character, and choice. These
three C's must now supplement the three R's.

The discussion about excellence in American education is
well under way. The federal government has contributed to the
dialogue by urging high standards. The very first recommendation
of Secretary of Education Terrel Bell's National Commission on
Excellence in Education was that *every* high school student receive a common education. The commission recommended four
years of English, three years of math, three years of science, and
three years of history and social studies. This is where we must
look as we discuss the first "C": content.

We shift and change what we ask our students to learn from
year to year. There seems to be a new educational fad for every
new class. Though educators are distressed when students lack

* This chapter is based on an address delivered to the National Press Club,
Washington, D.C., March 27, 1985.

commitment to their studies, it could be that students are simply following the example many educators have set. We are trend-crazy. Where is the stick-to-it-iveness, not of students but of educators?

Good teaching does more than teach skills. Skills are important, but knowledge is at least as important, and knowledge can come only from content. Surely one of our highest charges in teaching is to teach what we ourselves have loved—such as *The Call of the Wild, Treasure Island, Swiss Family Robinson, Huckleberry Finn.* If we remove this kind of content from our courses, we take away the very things that make students love to be students, and that lead to the improvement of skills. Or, as Diane Ravitch has asked, Who ever heard of a child staying up at night reading a basic reader? At present American education is long on technique and short on tradition. But technique without tradition is empty.

What should our children know? George Orwell somewhere said that often it is the first duty of intelligent men to restate the obvious. So let me aspire to suggest the shape of the obvious, starting with the humanities in our schools. It is important to know what justice is, what courage is. It is important to know what is noble and what is base. It is important to know what deserves to be defended, and what deserves to be loved. In the words of Montaigne, it is important to know the difference between ambition and greed, between loyalty and servitude, between liberty and license.

And more. Every student should know how mountains are made, and that for every action there is an equal and opposite reaction. They should know who said "I am the state" and who said "I have a dream." They should know about subjects and predicates, about isosceles triangles and ellipses. They should know where the Amazon flows, and what the First Amendment means. They should know about the Donner party and slavery, and Shylock, Hercules, and Abigail Adams, where Ethiopia is, and why there is a Berlin Wall. They should know a little of how a poem works, how a plant works, and what it means to remark "If wishes were horses, beggars would ride." They should know the place of the Milky Way and DNA in the unfolding of the universe. They should know something about the Constitutional Convention of

1787 and about the conventions of good behavior. They should know a little of what the Sistine Chapel looks like and what great music sounds like.

Our students should know our nation's ideals and aspirations. We believe in liberty and equality, in limited government and the betterment of the human condition. These truths underlie our society, and though they may be self-evident, they are not spontaneously apprehended by the young. Our students should know these ideals, and they should know that a large part of the world thinks and acts according to other beliefs.

These are things we should want *all* our students to know. We should not hold some students to lesser goals, pushing them into educational backwaters while everyone else is advancing upstream. Albert Shanker, president of the American Federation of Teachers, once asked a class of average and less than average students: What should we ask you to read? After a pause one student raised his hand. "Mr. Shanker," he asked, "what do the smart kids read?"

Not all students have the same abilities, so it is up to our teachers to adapt good material to the level of the student. Good teachers will vary the pedagogy, of course—use books, tapes, or films or tell stories—but they will also retain the substance. Whatever the pedagogy, they must not lose the substance. In certain places in America, there has sometimes been a great zeal to remove certain topics from study. Let us match that zeal for exclusion with a zeal for inclusion.

Whatever disagreements we may have about the specific nature of content, most of us believe that content is central to education. Nor should there be much argument on the central importance of the second "C": character.

Americans have always believed that in education the development of intellect and character go hand in hand. What is character? My dictionary defines it as "strength of mind, individuality, independence, moral quality." We could, of course, include more: thoughtfulness, fidelity, kindness, honesty, respect for law, standards of right and wrong, diligence, fairness, and self-discipline.

But how can these qualities be taught? It seems many of our

schools have forgotten the answer. In recent years, although we have not overintellectualized the curriculum, ironically we have tried to intellectualize moral development. Many have turned to a whole range of "values education" theories and practices where the goal is to guide children in developing their own values by discussion, dialogue, simulation, even games.

While it is true that good character can have an intellectual aspect, the development of intellect has never guaranteed the development of good character. (Germany in the 1930s was intellectually advanced.) Aristotle knew, and psychologists confirm today, that it is habit which develops virtues, habit shaped not only by precept but by example as well. "It makes no small difference," Aristotle wrote, "whether we form habits of one kind or of another from our very youth; it makes a very great difference, or rather *all* the difference." It is by exposing our children to good character and inviting its imitation that we will transmit to them a moral foundation.

Teaching character begins where it must—in the home, starting with those early childhood years from infancy to age six. But after that our schools must help. And a school must have character if it is to transmit character to its students.

First, teachers and principals must be willing to articulate ideals and convictions to students. As Oxford's Mary Warnock has written, "You cannot teach morality without being committed to morality yourself; and you cannot be committed to morality yourself without holding that some things are right and others wrong." Second, the character of a school, its *ethos*, is determined not only by the articulation of ideals and convictions, but by the behavior of authorities. We must have principals and teachers who know the difference between right and wrong, good and bad, and who themselves exemplify high moral purpose.

Students cannot be browbeaten into accepting points of view. That would simply be indoctrination, which we all deplore. I am talking about intellectual honesty and ethical candor. To put students in the presence of a morally mature adult who speaks honestly to them is the surest way to foster their moral growth. In building character, nothing is as important as the quiet power of moral example.

The character of a school is also determined by the kind of

place it is. Here I am speaking of the physical and moral tone of the school premises—again, its ethos. School effectiveness studies have shown over and over again the importance of both these elements. A school with broken windowpanes, graffitied walls, and littered floors is a school that has failed one of its own lessons. A disorderly environment is bound to affect morale. Plato tells us in the *Republic* that the stamp of baseness on a building will sink deep into the souls of those it surrounds.

And there are, of course, more insidious forms of disorderliness. One is called drug abuse, and that includes alcoholism. The student chosen by the National Association of Secondary School Principals as the outstanding student leader of 1985 said the biggest problem confronting our schools is teenage alcoholism. "Everywhere you look, there's liquor," he said.

Orderliness must prevail in a school aspiring to transmit good character. Only a school run in a disciplined manner can teach self-discipline to students. As the sociologist Amitai Etzioni has recently pointed out, a lack of self-discipline might be our students' greatest failure, the cause of so many other failures. The problem of school character demands our teachers' and principals' deepest commitment to moral example and discipline.

There is one specific initiative that should be mentioned. President Charles W. Eliot of Harvard once said that "in the campaign for character no auxiliaries are to be refused." Might not voluntary school prayer be an auxiliary to character? I believe it can be. In any case, I do not believe the federal government should decide, a priori, whether school prayer may or may not be allowed. I do not believe that *voluntary* prayer in school should be prohibited, as it is today.

As any parent knows, teaching character is a difficult task. But it is a crucial task because we want our children to be not only healthy, happy, and successful but decent, strong, and good. None of this happens automatically; there is no genetic transmission of virtue. It takes conscious, committed effort. It takes attention. We must give it more.

Almost all of us, then, agree on the importance of both content and character in education. But in the search for schools of content and character many parents are frustrated. And this brings us to our third "C": choice.

Not all teachers are parents, but all parents are teachers, the all but indispensable teachers. And as teachers, parents always have had the first and largest responsibility for educating their children. Starting in the nineteenth century, citizens in all states acted through their legislatures to create the public school systems that the overwhelming majority of children attend today. The fact that we have established public schools is not a surrender by parents of their basic responsibility for education. Each parent still has that responsibility. The public school system exists to serve the parent and the child by performing the specific jobs entrusted to it.

What do parents expect of the school? We expect the teachers in the school to teach our children things we might not know, like how to speak French or the causes of the Russian Revolution. And things we may have forgotten, like exactly what the Stamp Act was or how to find a square root. In general, we expect the school to teach our children the things that we ourselves, as parents, would want to teach them if we had the time and the knack and the knowledge. We also hope and expect that the schools will perform this task reasonably well.

The problem today is not only that some schools fail parents' expectations, but also that such schools cannot be held accountable by those they are supposed to serve. Accountability could be improved if parents were able to choose another school—a better school. Unfortunately, the majority of American parents do not have the freedom to make this choice. Some do. The affluent can buy the school of their choice by buying a house in the neighborhood of their choice. But the great majority of Americans are not wealthy, though they too are the heirs to a great promise—American public education's promise that it will provide the education parents wish for their children.

Parental frustration with particular public schools is now widespread. Many parents realize their children are not learning enough. Or, more disheartening, they discover that their children are unlearning in school lessons they have been taught at home. A concern for the beliefs and values that have been nurtured within the family sometimes seems to fall on deaf ears. In some schools parents are simply not taken seriously. As columnist William Raspberry has said, "Parental involvement means parents are expected to show up to do what they are told when the principal invites them, or prepare a dish for a pot-luck dinner, or come to PTA meetings a couple of times a year." More than anything else, parents need to be able to choose environments that affirm their principles. They need to find schools where their own values will not be lost or distorted.

Nothing should be higher on the national agenda than the improvement of our public schools. Many are improving; and they should be applauded. Improvement can be aided by redesigning public education to ensure accountability through instruments of choice—instruments that will, in turn, enable parents to fulfill *their* responsibility for their children's education. We must offer parents instruments of choice within public education and between public and private education. It is ironic that the American system of higher education, with generous taxpayer support, provides such choice in the selection of colleges, while in elementary and secondary education, which is compulsory for all, there is choice for so few. All parents, not only the affluent, must be able to exercise greater choice in what, where, and how their children learn.

Education is and should always remain primarily a state and local responsibility. In finding new instruments of choice, the states must be the laboratories of experimentation. Some are already using systems that encourage choice, and others are exploring new plans. Developing instruments of choice will not lead to a mass exodus from the public schools; on the contrary, it will lead to a significant benefit for all schools. For those public schools that have been holding a captive audience, competition will be one of the best catalysts to make them improve their performance. Freedom of choice must not be bound by economic lines. All parents must have the opportunity to hold the system accountable so that they can fulfill their responsibility for their children's education. As Professor John Coons of the University of California Law School at Berkeley has written, we will know that those in public education "are serious about reform when they are at last prepared to cede to the ordinary family the authority that has so well served those of us who could afford to choose our schools."

My agenda is a limited one. Specific policy recommendations are inherently and properly limited by the fact that education in America always has been, and always should be, a local and state responsibility. Real reform in our schools cannot come from inside the Department of Education in Washington. It has to come from inside our schools and our communities. That is why I am pressing for the three C's—content, character, and choice—in American education. I believe that the ideas they represent deserve the nation's attention, for nothing less than the sake of our children's future.

First Lessons:
American
Elementary Education[*]

MY REPORT *First Lessons*, is the first general report the country has seen on the performance of its elementary schools since 1953. In the intervening years—in recent years particularly—we've heard a lot about secondary education, and a good deal about higher education. But concerning the performance of our elementary schools, not enough has been said.

Next to the family, elementary school is arguably the most influential institution in our children's lives. In elementary school children gain—or do not gain—the skills that they will need throughout their school years, and throughout their adult lives. Elementary school is where they gain (or do not gain) fundamental knowledge of themselves, and of our country and common heritage. It is also where they develop (or do not develop) the personal qualities—the habits, values, and demeanor—they will carry with them for the rest of their lives.

In short, elementary school plays a central role in deciding the fundamental issue of how we raise, educate, nurture, and protect our children. This is something in which all of us—not just parents, teachers, and principals—have an interest. Wordsworth said the "Child is the father of the Man." The education that we give our

[*] This chapter is based on an address delivered to the National Press Club, Washington, D.C., September 2, 1986.

children—in school and out—affects in no small measure the character of our future adults. It affects the character of our society as a whole, for better or for worse.

When our children are well educated in the early years, a great number of social problems can be averted far ahead of time. A child who cannot read when he leaves the eighth grade is a much more likely candidate for the unemployment line or the police lineup than his classmates who can read. If prevention is the best medicine, then attending to the well-being of our elementary schools is crucial to all of us.

Right now, we tend as a nation to attach more importance to other levels of education. Every year our colleges and universities receive billions of dollars in donations; the troubles in our high schools have been explored in a host of reports and analyses. We must come to understand that education is not a hierarchy. It is a continuum, lasting a lifetime. Without a solid foundation in the elementary years, it cannot possibly succeed.

First Lessons is the first comprehensive examination of the nation's elementary schools in a third of a century. How are they performing? On the whole, not badly—pretty well, in fact. There is no rising tide of mediocrity flooding our elementary schools. Indeed, the Congressional Budget Office recently concluded that "achievement in the elementary grades is now by some measures at its highest level in three decades." In the first few grades especially, things look good. Most of our youngest students are learning to read, to write, and to perform basic mathematical functions.

But something seems to happen between the first few grades of elementary school and its conclusion. In general, as our elementary students get older, their performance begins to decline. And by the time they reach the upper grades—as we know from data gathered in international comparisons—they lag behind students from other nations in mathematics, reading, and other areas.

The most sublime, the most solemn responsibility of our elementary schools is to teach children to read. When a school graduates a child who cannot read, that school has failed in its responsibility to the child and to the community. Studies show that today's elementary schoolchildren are better readers than those of fifteen years ago. According to the latest study by the National Assessment of Educational Progress, nearly 94 percent of nine-year-olds today possess rudimentary reading skills: they are able to follow written directions; they can match a picture with a written description. Yet, as they grow older, their performance falls well below what we should expect. According to the National Assessment of Educational Progress report, 40 percent of thirteen-year-olds lack the intermediate reading skills necessary to handle the books and lessons that we would expect a seventh- or eighth-grade teacher to assign. Most minority children fall below that intermediate level.   .

Teaching children to read is not a mysterious science. We know how it's done. We do it successfully all the time. We know, for instance, that children get a valuable start when their parents or other adults read to them at home. It helps when they are exposed to books from an early age. We know that a mixture of formal and informal instruction may be undertaken as early as kindergarten.

And we know that for most children, the most effective method for teaching reading is that which first teaches children the relationship between letters and sounds. This method is known as "phonics." From the 1920s to the early 1970s, a method known as "look-say" prevailed in our schools. It relied on children's memorizing the appearance of entire words. This method has proven considerably less effective than phonics.

Perhaps most important in teaching reading is the simple fact that children learn to read by reading. Books should occupy a central place in the home and the classroom; they should always be within children's reach. We should make sure that every schoolchild has a library card—and uses it.

Finally, let's make sure the books we provide our children are well written and interesting. Children may be discouraged from reading by the deadening prose and content of texts currently assigned in our elementary schools. Given our rich cultural heritage, this is inexcusable. Schools should compete for the attention of the mind and heart by offering the best that we have. Let's have our children read books like *Where the Wild Things Are,* *Winnie the Pooh,* and *Swiss Family Robinson.*

Another area in which there is considerable need for improvement is social studies. Social studies should be the means by which we introduce children to our world and to our common culture. We want our children to learn of the events, people, and ideas that define us as a nation and as a civilization. By the end of the eighth grade, we should expect our children to know the basic saga of American history and the stories of its great men and women; they should know how our form of government works and have some understanding of the principles on which it is based; they should know the contours and locations of the physical world, and essential facts about the world's major nations; they should have a basic grasp of their rights and obligations as American citizens.

Yet many of today's children pick up only bits and pieces of these lessons. In a recent international survey, 20 percent of the American twelve-year-olds in one test group could not find the United States on a map. Another study showed that only half our seventeen-year-olds could place the Civil War in the correct half-century. Our children are failing to learn these important lessons in part because they are submerged in a mass of extraneous information, derived from disciplines like anthropology, sociology, law, economics, and psychology. Instead of "social studies," young children are being taught social science and social living. And they are being denied an introduction to their own heritage.

Social studies as it now exists should be transformed. I suggest that we teach the knowledge and skills needed for life in a democratic society through three interrelated disciplines, the three pillars upon which our elementary-school social studies curricula should be based: history, geography, and civics.

In history, our children should learn not only the dates of major events in United States and world history but also their significance. They should be able to identify great men and women of the past, and be familiar with fundamental documents like the Declaration of Independence and the Constitution. In geography, they should learn the basic themes stressed in geography texts: place, relationships between places, movement, location, and regions. They should be able to identify the major nations of the world. Civics and history are fundamental. The proper focus of American schoolchildren is on the essential facts, the central institutions, and the fundamental principles of the United States and the Western civilization whose culture and tradition are our shared inheritance.

In the sciences, too, we should make major changes in our instructional approach. Right now, our teaching of science is at odds with its true nature. We have come to think of science as a collection of esoteric facts and stunts—the periodic table, the innards of frogs, the way to make little hot plates out of wires. But science is a method of reasoning that applies not just to investigations of the physical universe, but to every intellectual inquiry requiring hypothesis, inference, and other tools of brainwork. It is a method young students will need for an ordered adventure through the world of knowledge.

Elementary school children would benefit, too, from more "hands on" exploration in science. Seen as a list of theorems in a book, science can be a bore. But as a practical adventure guided by a knowledgeable teacher, it can sweep children up in the excitement of discovery. Consider, for instance, Anne Beers School in Washington, D.C. This school designated an entire wing of the building as its science center. At any time of the day, children can be found there peering through microscopes, digging into dirt samples, or discussing the differences between jungles and forests. They are learning science by doing science.

The education of a child extends well beyond the elementary school classroom—it extends to the home, and to neighbors' and friends' homes; to the local shopping center and to the movie theater; to wherever it is that child spends his or her time, to whatever and to whomever he or she meets. In short, the education of future generations is something in which we all not only have a stake—it is something in which we all play a part and in which we all have a responsibility.

We cannot afford to regard education as the exclusive concern of parents and professional educators. Parents and teachers must be able to draw on the expertise and example of other adults—of family members, friends and neighbors, church members, doctors, policemen, social workers, clergymen, and coaches. Our culture depends on it. Our children depend on it. If our institutions, values, and knowledge are to make it into the next century in good shape, we must come to regard the education of the young as a task shared by all of us, by an entire community of responsible adults.

THREE

Educating
Disadvantaged Children*

GARRISON ELEMENTARY SCHOOL is a school that works, and it works in circumstances where many believe schools cannot work. Garrison kids are from the Bronx and don't have all the advantages; in fact, many students here don't have many advantages other than Garrison itself. But that's enough. In Garrison and schools like it, something is being achieved that is very important to Americans. What is achieved in these places is important both in the field of education and beyond the field of education. Americans need to know about the success of Garrison and schools like it.

Among the schools I have visited as Secretary of Education I have seen many, like Garrison, that are succeeding against the socioeconomic odds. Charles Rice Elementary School serves one of the most disadvantaged neighborhoods in Dallas. The school's motto is "Excellent Behavior, Excellent Academics." In 1984, as part of a court-ordered desegregation agreement intended to reduce the amount of busing, grades four through six were added to the school. Under the agreement, the school dedicated itself to raising the reading scores of children in those grades by 10 percentile points each year. The principal, Louise Smith, and her staff met that goal. In 1987, they pledged to do the same in math. Louise

* This chapter is based on an address delivered to Garrison Elementary Schools, The Bronx, New York, January 13, 1987.

Smith *knows* each of the children in her school, and they have become children eager to learn and confident that they can do so. When I asked the children in a third-grade class how many of them were going to college, *every* hand went up.

In the fall of 1986, I visited Lee Elementary School in one of Milwaukee's poorest neighborhoods, another school succeeding against the odds. The principal, George Hughes, carries a portable telephone as he moves throughout the school, and when he sees a student "doing good," he often calls the child's parents on the spot to tell them. The school fosters student achievement and provides special recognition for homework completion and good conduct.

I have also had the pleasure of meeting the students and staff of P.S. 189, a bilingual school in Brooklyn. Ninety-five percent of the students come from low-income families; more than two-thirds are from immigrant families whose native language is not English. Those students learn English, and students whose native language is English also learn a second language. The principal of P.S. 189, Jo Bruno, and her staff have 91 percent of their students performing at or above grade level in math, 86 percent in reading.

In the Bronx, Dallas, Milwaukee, and Brooklyn, these schools work, and there are common reasons for their success. These schools have outstanding principals who lead and inspire and bring out the best from dedicated, motivated teaching staffs. These schools reach out to parents and establish an alliance of home, community, and school—an alliance dedicated to the nurture, protection, and education of children. These schools concentrate on the basics—good behavior and academic achievement—and set rigorous standards for children. These schools nurture character and transmit a clear sense of right and wrong. And these schools operate on the principle that all children can learn. They reward achievement, and they provide regular assessments of progress so the students can get the help and support they need. They don't focus on failure, and they don't get failure. They focus on success, and they usually get success.

I am struck by the fact that the success of schools like Garrison, Charles Rice, Lee, and P.S. 189 is frequently obscured. Some like to think of them as "exceptions," as happy exceptions indeed but exceptions nonetheless, to a general pattern of hopelessness in deprived communities. But I think of them not as exceptions, but as instances of a rule: the rule that good education *is* possible for all of our children. The rules of good education are pretty much the same all over; they work at schools in the suburbs and in the South Bronx. Failing to recognize these schools' success, and the reasons for their success, hinders our ability to foster more such schools.

Part of the reason that we have not fully appreciated what is being accomplished by these schools is that their achievements do not fit the existing categories of our public policy debate. Conservatives have, I think, been correct in general about what makes for good education—such things as standards, discipline, basics, strong leadership, and high expectations. But conservatives have paid insufficient attention in the past to the education of the disadvantaged. They did not, on the whole, direct their efforts specifically to the question of what works for *these* children. Conservatives are strong advocates for families; but only recently have they begun translating this broad concern into policies that speak specifically to the well-being of children growing up in poor families.

Liberals, on the other hand, have been vocal advocates of eliminating discrimination and improving the lives of the poor. They deserve credit for this. But they have often advocated ineffective—I would even say counterproductive—means. Liberals seem to believe that unless the government can somehow fundamentally transform the conditions under which disadvantaged children live, those children cannot be expected to succeed in school. Liberals also tend to assume that disadvantaged children need an education that is different from the education of others, from the traditional emphasis on the basics of behavior and academics; and they have sometimes argued that it is unfair to hold disadvantaged children to rigorous standards. So on this side, there has been much by way of good intentions—but there has also been much wrong-headedness.

The good intentions of all Americans have made possible important strides in the education of the disadvantaged in recent decades. In 1950, fully one-quarter of all black children of high school age were not officially enrolled in school. By 1980, enrollment in high school was effectively universal, and racial disparities in enrollment had entirely disappeared. This is good. We should be proud of our progress in expanding the access to education of disadvantaged children. And we should focus even greater attention on the fact that education for the disadvantaged is an extraordinarily effective means of escaping poverty. Common sense tells us this, and social science research confirms it.

Unfortunately, while we have increased access to education for disadvantaged students, in too many instances the dropout rate for schools serving such students has been increasing. Academic performance in such schools generally remains low. And painful as it may be to admit, many of the well-intentioned reforms advanced in the 1960s and '70s contributed to the problem. Educators promoted novel experiments, often with the best of motives; but when these experiments failed, it was usually disadvantaged children—those most dependent for their future prospects on good schooling—who paid the highest price. When schools were encouraged to become "value-free," when emphasis on the basics was challenged in favor of freeing children's "innate wisdom" in "open classrooms," and when reliable methods of measuring achievement were jettisoned on the assumption that homework, tests, and grades were needlessly oppressive—in each of these cases, it was disadvantaged children who were harmed the most.

So, at the very same time that we were extending the ladder of educational opportunity to the disadvantaged, we were hindering their ability to climb that ladder. For in the end, we need to do two things: We need to provide the ladder, and also to foster and develop individuals' ability and motivation to climb the rungs. This means attending to the habits, skills, attitudes, and values of these children so they may climb it. We have not done this as conscientiously as we should have.

As a result, some today seem to believe we can no longer expect disadvantaged children to achieve the way other children do. Much of the earlier optimism has turned to despair. There is a belief that we face a permanent underclass whose children cannot be expected to learn much or to be helped much by our schools.

Fortunately, we not only have extensive research on the characteristics of schools that effectively educate disadvantaged children, we also have the concrete example of schools such as the ones I've mentioned. What makes them tick? What is their secret for success? What are the rules they embody?

There are three key traits. First, these schools are *anti-determinist*. That is, these schools act on the premise that no immutable law dooms a poor or disadvantaged child to failure simply because he is poor or disadvantaged. These schools believe they can make a difference, their staffs and teachers act as if they can make a difference, and believing and acting in this way, they do make a difference. They dote on their pupils, they help get them on their feet and point them the way up. Garrison Elementary, Charles Rice, Lee Elementary, P.S. 189, and many other successful schools are remarkably alike in this respect. P.S. 189's principal Jo Bruno's slogan is "Everyone Can Learn." A Garrison school teacher says, "Children here are *somebody*; we know they can succeed," and one of her students exclaims, "My mother says, '*This* is a school.'" At Eastside High School in Paterson, New Jersey, another school succeeding against the odds, a parent told her child simply, "You go there and you *will* learn."

Second, these schools approach education from a distinctly *anti-relativist* point of view. They do not fall into the error of relativism—that is, the belief that values cannot be generalized, because they are different for rich and poor, for black and white. These schools do not neglect or deny differences in culture and background; far from it—they affirm them. But they do not let such differences hinder the education of their children to a common enabling standard. P.S. 189's Mrs. Bruno says that "the students come in and tell us that they are special; we in turn have to treat them as special." But for her school and others like it, "special" doesn't mean lower standards or lesser expectations. Special means exposing these students to a challenging curriculum—to nothing less than the best our society has to offer.

Finally, these good schools are *anti-faddish*. These schools *know* what works; they scorn educational fads and insist on fundamentals. If there are failed tests, poor teaching skills, low student performance, or high suspension rates, these schools know what to do. They don't complain; they act. Their answer is more testing, better teachers, lots of homework, longer hours, tougher discipline, a clean and orderly building, more motivation for achievement. They stress the basics—reading, mathematics, writing—and use every means they can to support and strengthen the basics. In an evaluation report on P.S. 189, a site visitor wrote: "In all the classrooms the teacher was the dominant figure. Classrooms were old-fashioned in design. Desks and chairs were in straight rows. Teachers called on students and students responded. Everything seemed old and outdated, yet the students are motivated, happy, and productive." These schools communicate the essentials of the common American culture: geography, history, literature, and democratic principles. They set goals and objectives for students in precise and measurable terms. In other words, they teach an "intellectual work ethic," in what some might disparagingly call "the old-fashioned way." But you can't disparage their results.

At Garrison Elementary, students get up to three hours of solid reading a day; they are also exposed to subjects like art, history, drama, and meteorology. In short, the school doesn't fool around. One little girl explains: "In other schools, they don't *teach* you. You do what you want to do, and they let you pass. In this school, if you don't learn, they put you back. *They give you more here.*" Schools like these demand effort, good conduct, and self-discipline. These hard values are at the heart of their success.

The stories of these schools point the way to a redirection of education policy in general. Education policy should have a simple goal: to produce more, many more, such schools. These schools and their principals and teachers are doing nothing less than saving lives. In large measure they are realizing the sound liberal goals of the sixties and seventies. But they are doing this by employing what we could call profoundly conservative means, by the vital and creative and humane application of old values in new settings. For too long the successes of these schools have been ignored by both liberals and conservatives. But in them, liberal idealism and conservative realism meet.

About fifteen years ago, Harvard professor Nathan Glazer entitled a book of essays *Remembering the Answers.* His point was that in the 1960s many people forgot—or willfully rejected—the most basic and sensible answers to first questions, to the questions about what contributes to social well-being and prosperity, about what makes for individual character and responsibility, and, yes, happiness.

The recovery of this knowledge offers real hope for the poor.

It treats the poor with dignity—as responsible individuals and not as permanent dependents of government. It also reminds us of truths we all know from personal experience—what we know privately but don't often enough say publicly. I am thinking of truths like this: that the nurture of character and the promotion of rigorous standards of performance in our schools are the necessary foundation of good education and the best preparation for adult life. We have a duty to affirm *publicly* the truths that we know *privately*. In recent years, these truths have had little relation to our public policy or even our public discourse. Policymakers must now attend more forthrightly to the somewhat abstract but nonetheless crucial realm of principles and beliefs, attitudes and values. It is the focus on these principles, beliefs, attitudes and values— and on people who hold them—that is, I believe, the secret of success of Garrison and other schools like it. It is to the principles and values these schools embody that we must look for broader efforts in public policy.

We know what works in the education of the disadvantaged. We have focused too long on what has not worked. This has led some to something close to despair. But we need not despair. It is true that if we focus on failure, we are likely to get failure. But if we focus on success, we shall get success. And our task is to study the success stories, to publicize them, to replicate them, and to fashion public policies that foster, encourage, and reward success. We now have a historic opportunity to provide a good education to all children in this nation. And for disadvantaged children in particular, a good education is crucial if they are to gain access to the full measure of opportunities offered by this great nation.

PART
TWO

LET US
NOW
PRAISE

FOUR

Let Us Now Praise
Good Schools *

FIVE YEARS AGO Eastside High School in Paterson, New Jersey, was an inner-city school that had simply gone out of control. Gangs roamed the hallways carrying razors and knives to extort money from other students. Hoodlums recruited girls for prostitution. Drug dealing was rampant and open; the smell of dope filled the stairwells.

On a typical day at Eastside High, one-third of the student body was either absent or on suspension. Students wandered in and out of classrooms whenever they felt like it. Vandalism was commonplace. More than 60 percent of the tenth-grade class was functionally illiterate.

On the first day of school in 1981, a student stabbed a security guard. Teachers had been attacked and beaten. The county prosecutor's office called Eastside "a caldron of violence and terror" and recommended that the place be permanently shut down.

This school was not unique. But it was as bad a situation as you are going to find in any school, anywhere, anytime. It was the kind of situation where people simply give up hope. It was the kind of place people point to when they want an example of a failed public school.

* This chapter is based on an address delivered to the National School Boards Association, Las Vegas, Nevada, April 5, 1986.

Joe Clark volunteered to take over in 1982. On the morning of September 8, opening day at Eastside High, three thousand students found Clark waiting in the hall with a bullhorn in his hand. "I am your new principal, Joe Clark," he said. "This is the *new* Eastside High School. What was, exists no more. Get to your classrooms."

Everyone was given a list of rules. If you talked back to a teacher, you were suspended for five days. If you graffitied a wall, ten days. Clark announced a dress code. "You've got Calvin Kleins on your behinds and nothing in your minds," he said. The school was cleaned from top to bottom. Security guards were put in the stairwells.

If a teacher was incompetent, Clark told him so to his face. Twenty transferred out. Three hundred juniors and seniors were expelled. "I'm not going to let three hundred hoodlums destroy the lives of three thousand students," Clark told them. As for drugs, he told students: "If you're smoking or dealing, you're out." And he put pushers on notice: "If you come here, you just might get hurt."

Joe Clark asked his students to memorize the alma mater and be prepared to sing it, if asked, over the public address system. Every morning he announced the names of students who had done something well. Clark exhorted and he cajoled. "Just because you're poor doesn't mean you have to be a thug or a hoodlum," he told them. "Neglect your education, and you're finished." He let students know that he believed in them, and what he expected of them. He was everywhere, all over the school. One morning he strapped a pedometer to his ankle and discovered he had walked twenty miles by the end of the day.

Today Eastside High is a different school. In 1981, 56 percent of the ninth-graders passed the New Jersey minimum basic skills test in math. By 1984, the figure was 91 percent. The reading test rate rose from 40 to 68 percent. SAT scores are up. Violence and drugs are gone. Enrollment is up, attendance is good. And, perhaps most promising of all, neighborhood kids are coming back. Middle-class children are coming back to Eastside from the parochial and private schools. That's right—parental choice is resulting in movement from private schools to a public school, a public school that once was, but is no more, a caldron of violence and terror.

You can make the argument that one man cleaned up East-side High. But you also have to keep in mind what Socrates says in Plato's *Gorgias:* You can't be a good citizen alone. Someone had to be behind Joe Clark, backing him, supporting him, giving him the power to do what he had to do. That someone was, at least in part, the school board. But another important thing was happening: the community of parents was increasingly involved in activities at the school.

Can this kind of story be replicated? Or are there some schools where we just have to give up? Joe Clark says others can do it. And in fact we know others have done it. There are numerous success stories—public schools that have been turned around like Eastside High, some that are getting better, some that have always managed to be good. I have praised not only schools that have won the Education Department's School Recognition Program award, but some others as well that have come a long way to become places of learning and respect.

These are stories that we should not hesitate to hold up to praise. More important, these are stories from which we must learn lessons. To paraphrase St. Paul: Whatsover things are true, whatsoever things are lovely, whatsoever things are of good report, if there be any virtue, and if there be any praise, think on these things. To put it another way, if we focus on failure, we might get it. And if we focus on success, we might get it.

There are some things on which not everyone agrees—the appropriate size of the federal education budget, for example. Or the question of parental choice through, for example, school vouchers. This is not surprising; reasonable people may certainly disagree over these matters. But on some things we should all be able to agree, things we *must* agree on for the sake of our schools. Because without them our schools cannot succeed, no matter how much money the federal government or anyone else spends. We proved that, I think, during the sixties and seventies.

A new report called "The Search for Successful Secondary Schools" examines 571 winners in the Education Department's Secondary School Recognition Program to find out what makes these good schools tick. It's an important study for a couple of reasons. First, because it's one more nail in the coffin of educational dopiness. The findings here are not especially surprising—they should not be especially surprising—because they are consistent with common sense. But in the last two decades common sense has often been beaten, shoved, and kicked around. Second, the study is important because the findings are consistent with the major themes of the "effective schools" research of the past decade that was done on elementary schools. And the things that make schools good at one level seem to work at another level. This study finds the same attributes showing up in exemplary secondary schools.

The first attribute is *good principals*. Quite simply, good schools have good principals. The two go hand in hand. A good principal can make a good school out of a bad school. When I asked Joe Clark if he was one of a kind, he looked at me and said, "That's a bunch of balderdash." And he's right.

Take, for example, the individuals who turned around Artesia High School in Lakewood, California. Seventy percent of Artesia's students are from low-income families. Forty-two percent are white, 36 percent are Hispanic, and 19 percent are Asian. A few years ago, Artesia's reputation was bad. The school was gang-ridden. One-fourth of the students were absent on any given day. Many children were simply afraid to go to school. Scores were low. Realtors were reluctant to sell homes in the area to anyone with children.

The summer before their first year on the job, the new principal, Mara Clisby, and the assistant principal for discipline, Joseph Quarles (who later became the principal), walked into the neighborhoods and into the homes of Artesia's gang leaders. They told both parents and students: It's over. No more gang warfare. Not at this school. They gave students a new discipline code. Any two students caught fighting were immediately suspended. But anyone joining a fight, anyone turning it into a gang fight, was gone for good. Period.

Mara Clisby moved her desk into the girls' bathroom, and she held her meetings and counseling there, just to stay visible. She put out a parents' handbook and invited parents into the school.

She instituted a citizenship code. She convinced teachers to ask more of students, and students to ask more of themselves.

Two years ago, Artesia High won our Secondary School Recognition Program award. In 1981, 54 percent of the graduates were going to college; by 1983, it had risen to 80 percent. Average daily attendance rose to 99 percent. The gang problems have disappeared. Artesia is now a model school.

Melvin Jones at Clara Westropp Middle School in Cleveland is one more principal who turned around a school. Clara Westropp is in a white-collar, affluent neighborhood. But most of the students are bused in from seventeen miles away. Ninety percent are from low-income families. Clara Westropp had four principals during the four years before Melvin Jones arrived. In academic achievement it was ranked last out of twenty-four schools in the district.

If you want to reach Melvin Jones in his office, you had better call between six-thirty and eight in the morning. The rest of the time, he's walking and talking. He says that "children have to see, hear, smell, and touch you, or else they start doing bad things." He's there watching when they get off the buses every morning. He shoots basketball with them.

"I give my kids a sense of pride, kinship, and ownership," he says. "I teach my children, this is your book, your chair, your bus, your school." He has also been known to keep a pair of handcuffs in his desk. He says he's never used them, and never expects to. But the kids know that they are there.

Melvin Jones must be doing something right. Clara Westropp's athletics teams used to brawl when they lost and throw bricks at other teams' buses. Now, Jones says, they act like young ladies and gentlemen. And in four years, Clara Westropp rose academically from dead last to six out of the twenty-four schools in the district. Clara Westropp, by the way, is the fourth school that Melvin Jones has turned around.

At every good school you will find a good principal, and there are certain things these principals all stress. Foremost among them is the second attribute of good schools: *discipline*. It is hard to find a successful school without firm discipline. This is something we have always known, if not always heeded. A book called *Classroom*

Management, published in 1907, says: "There is no explicit formula that will cover each specific case, but one general suggestion may be given: *Get order.* Drop everything else, if necessary, until order is secured. Stretch your authority to the breaking point if you can do nothing else . . . you have the law back of you, you have intelligent public sentiment back of you."

We are not talking about merciless repression; we are not talking about authoritarianism; we *are* talking about an informing authority. We are talking about letting children know you care—about authority with a human face. Joe Clark is an authority, no doubt about it. But Clark also knows his students' names. He likes to know how their families are doing, and what their plans are for college or work. Artesia High's Joseph Quarles says that people told him he'd have nothing but enemies at the school. "But as long as the students know you are being fair with them, they don't hold it against you," he says. "Even the gang members admitted that I was being fair."

The third attribute of successful schools is *good teachers.* Again, no surprise. Our report finds that successful schools recruit and hold on to good teachers. And they reward teacher accomplishment. They single out good teachers to be honored by their peers, and they often show appreciation by giving merit pay, stipends for professional development, and promotions.

What makes a good teacher? When I talk to teachers and principals, I generally hear three criteria mentioned over and over again. Good teachers are people who know the subject matter well, are of sound character, and have the ability to communicate with young people. These, I think, are the necessary ingredients.

I like Joe Clark's philosophy: Accept no incompetence. Period. He told teachers that if they were incompetent they would leave in one of two ways, voluntarily or in a straitjacket (Joe pulls no punches), but that he would not let them ruin the education of those children. He heard a lot from the unions. Three union officials alone filed fifty personal grievances. Clark told a vice-principal to handle the grievances so he could do his job. Clark now has no bad teachers. Instead, for the first time in twenty years, teachers are lining up to teach at Eastside High.

Attribute number four is *high expectations, high standards.*

Virtually all of the ten high schools winning the Secondary School Recognition Program award have higher than average expectations and standards. They have high expectations regarding behavior and responsibility as well as academic achievement. And they stress homework. Schools that are good schools, and schools that are on their way to becoming good schools, expect a lot from their students.

Eastern High School in Washington, D.C., is an inner-city school in a black neighborhood, serving low- and middle-income students. Many of the good students in Eastern's area, and many of the children of the middle-class parents who can afford it, have been going to private or parochial schools. Ralph Neal, Eastern's principal, decided to change that.

Eastern traditionally had only grades ten through twelve. But in 1984 Ralph Neal created a special ninth-grade class to attract the best and brightest students from public, private, and parochial schools. The curriculum includes Latin, algebra, Shakespeare, and medieval history.

Forty-two students signed up for the program. But they were not the students Neal was looking for. They did not come from the parochial and private schools. Their reading and mathematics skills were generally below grade level. But they wanted to learn, and as one Eastern teacher said, "We dared not venture from giving these kids a chance to learn the material." So they modified the curriculum, and those children are learning Latin, Shakespeare, algebra, and history. The moral: Children—and parents—will answer the call of high expectations.

But the story doesn't end there. Ralph Neal didn't get the cream of the crop, but he's not giving up. He's going to continue the program. He says, "We're saying to parents on Capitol Hill that we have a good academic program, and that they won't need to go across town or out of the public school system to get a quality education. Once the word gets out, it's just a matter of time before we get bombarded with those middle-class families." As a matter of fact, word has gotten out. Parents have already met with Ralph Neal about moving their children from parochial schools to Eastern. Neal's high expectations and demanding curricula are sure to attract more students back to Eastern.

The fifth attribute of successful schools is *parental and community involvement*. Four out of five high schools winning the Secondary School Recognition Program award report above average or exceptional parental involvement. Good schools beg parents to give as much time and energy as they can to their children's education. And when schools work hard, parents respond.

Case in point: When Joe Clark decided that three hundred students with long records of suspensions and absenteeism would have to go, the local board of education held a meeting. One parent showed up to complain. Over four hundred parents showed up to support Joe Clark. "When a man is about good works," Clark says, "parents see the good things happening, and they say to their children: 'You go there, and you will learn.'"

The sixth and final attribute of successful schools is *ethos*. The "Search for Successful Schools" report calls it "positive school climate," but I prefer the Greek term for this over the educationese. The Greek word *ethos* originally meant "the habits of the animals in a place." In the context of successful schools, it means a certain spirit which a school embodies. It is its character. It is the configuration of values and goals that students, teachers, administrators, and parents share.

The ethos of a school is, in a way, the sum of everything I have talked about so far—all of the above. It is not easy to describe. But walk into a successful school and you will find a place that knows what it is about, that has a real, substantive vision of what an educated child should be like when he leaves that school. That, I think, is one reason it is often hard to find good principals in their offices. They have to be out, interacting with the children and teachers, giving the whole school that vision, being a man or woman who is good for the young to be around.

These, then, are some of the essential attributes that make good schools, public or private. The research tells us so. Common sense tells us so. We must pay attention to those things that make education work—that make it work even in difficult circumstances. We can't lose sight of the basics, the fundamental attributes without which we have seen so many schools decline.

Can we replicate the success stories sketched here? Yes, we can, if we heed the right kinds of things, if we ask the right questions, the fundamental ones. Those questions are: Who is in our schools and what are they teaching our children? That's the bottom line. All the rest is gloss.

There are many good schools, many success stories. Let us praise these schools and others. Let us concentrate on what is worthy of praise so that a year or two years or five years from now there will be many more schools worthy of praise.

FIVE

Let Us Now Praise Good Teachers *

A RECENT STUDY by the National Center for Education Information provided some keen insights into why people teach. According to NCEI director Emily Feistritzer, when asked what is most important to them on the job, teachers usually cite "a chance to use [their] minds and abilities" and "a chance to work with young people," followed by "appreciation for a job well done." Ninety-six percent of all teachers report that they love to teach. It is heartening to know that teachers are in the profession for all the reasons we hope they are.

Nevertheless, when it comes to appreciation—public appreciation—I think it is fair to assert that our good teachers deserve much wider recognition. Given the job they do, teachers deserve as much praise and thanks and honor as those in any other profession in our society. During my tenure as Secretary of Education I have spent a good deal of time inside classrooms. I have taught classes—third, seventh, and eleventh grades—and I have watched teachers in action. I have unbounded admiration for what good teachers do. It's hard work, teaching—among the hardest work I have done as Secretary of Education.

I have noticed, in my talks with people all over the country,

* This chapter is based on an address delivered to a rally of teachers from the Duval County public schools, Jacksonville, Florida, August 21, 1986.

that when I ask adults to name the individuals who have influenced their lives the most, they almost invariably mention a teacher. Somewhere along the line, there usually was a teacher who had a profound influence. And most of the time it was a teacher who was there in the early years. As Lee Iacocca wrote in his autobiography, "If you ask me the names of my professors in college or graduate school, I'd have trouble coming up with more than three or four. But I still remember the teachers who molded me in elementary and high school." And most Americans, I'm sure, would say the same thing.

I would like to offer the praise and respect due the teaching profession by suggesting three different senses in which teachers are indispensable to our identity as a nation, to the way we Americans think about ourselves as a people.

First, when we think about teaching, we think in terms of liberating each child's natural abilities, of nourishing those abilities and drawing them out so that the child can live up to his potential. To bring out what is best in an individual is one of the highest aims of teaching. To paraphrase Oliver Wendell Holmes, the teacher who is great is the teacher who makes others believe in greatness. Teaching is thus more than "facilitating the acquisition of skills." It is offering an invitation and encouragement to life, to a fulfilled life.

This idea of each of us fulfilling our potential also lies at the very heart of our American notions about self-government. Our faith in democracy is rooted in the belief that an individual can develop his natural abilities to the utmost only when he is free. It is not difficult, then, to see why Americans have traditionally placed such value on a good education and on good teachers. Education is the key to true freedom. In this sense, there is no one more important than teachers to the way of life and the system of government that Americans have chosen.

The second sense in which teachers are absolutely critical to our identity as a people lies in the fact that they hold the responsibility of preserving and transmitting to each new generation what may be called our "common culture," the things that bind Americans together as one people. In its highest form, this common culture is the sum of our intellectual and spiritual inheritance, our legacy from all the ages that have gone before us. It is the knowledge, ideas, and aspirations that shape our understanding of who we are as a people and what we are capable of.

What are some of these elements that make up our common culture? They are documents like the Constitution and the Declaration of Independence. They are certain principles, like the right to free speech and a belief that all men are created equal. They are the stories of certain individuals whose vision inspired a nation—towering figures like George Washington and Abraham Lincoln and Martin Luther King, Jr. They are events from our past that have shaped who we are, such as the landing of the *Mayflower*, the Boston Tea Party, the surrender at Appomattox, the landing at Normandy. Our common culture also consists of great books that give the highest kind of expression to the way we find ourselves in the world, ageless works like the *Odyssey* and *Macbeth* and *Huckleberry Finn*.

These are a few of the great milestones and achievements of our culture, and we should want all our children to know about them. More to the point, it is critical they know about them, for, as Walter Lippmann once observed, no culture can exist that is ignorant of its own traditions, its own inheritance.

Knowledge of these things is not spontaneously apprehended by the young. The common culture is not transmitted in our genes. The sense of who we are and the best we can be must be taught to each rising generation. This is the unique responsibility that teachers bear in preserving, protecting, and transmitting the common culture. For where else will the young turn for a reasoned and morally committed articulation of these things, if not to their teachers? Teachers are the trustees of our common culture.

Unfortunately, many of our schools are not doing all they can to transmit that common culture. In too many high schools, our students are never given the opportunity to read or at least to hear Shakespeare, or Homer, or to study closely *The Federalist* and the causes for which this nation was founded. This is a great loss. It is a loss for our students, of course, but also for our teachers, because transmitting our common culture is one of the noblest aspects of their profession. It is a responsibility and privilege that is uniquely theirs. And as my own teaching efforts have reminded me, passing on to others our enthusiasm for what we know and love is also one of the distinct joys of teaching. In short, when the content of what we teach our children is diluted, the special nature of the teaching vocation is diluted too.

The third sense in which teachers are indispensable to our identity as a people has to do with the fact that one of their most important jobs is to help shape the character of the young. For, as the ancient Greeks knew, the character of the entire *polis* ultimately depended on the character of its individual citizens. How we teach our children to conduct themselves and their affairs, and how we teach them to treat others, ultimately determines the kind of nation we are. A nation is as great as its people. Who molds people? Parents do. Teachers do.

As Secretary of Education, I have been trying to get the American people to think about not only the job teachers do but the kind of person it takes to do the job well. It seems to me that the public should expect three basic criteria of the people in front of their classrooms. First, all who teach our children should have a solid general education and know the material they plan to teach. Second, they should be of sound moral character. And third, they should like children, want to teach them, and be able to communicate knowledge and skills to them.

In return, we should be willing to give such a person our trust, our confidence, and a considerable amount of autonomy—more autonomy than many teachers have now. *Instructor* magazine recently surveyed several thousand elementary school teachers. Less than 30 percent said that they get to make "most" of the important decisions related to texts and supplementary materials for their students. Almost one-half said they make "none" of the important decisions related to teacher training in their schools. Sixty-one percent said they have no opportunities to observe their colleagues teaching. Only 24 percent said they were "meaningfully involved" in choosing the subjects and grades they teach.

In my opinion, this is no way to treat professionals. The American public—and school administrators—must remember that the teacher is the heart, and students the soul, of the educational enterprise. Schools are for teaching and learning first. All else is icing on the cake. The public should look carefully at how they treat their teachers, and at how much control teachers have over their own work. And local communities should look closely at their school budgets; because if you look at the public school dollar, you discover that the percentage that goes to teacher salaries has been steadily shrinking over the past decade—from 42 percent in 1973 to 37 percent in 1986. I think the public needs to make sure that, as they spend on their schools, they keep their priorities straight.

The public expects a lot from teachers. But by the same token, teachers should be able to expect the public to remember that they can't do their jobs alone. The education of a child is something to which many must contribute. There must be a sharing of labor among responsible adults. Parents, churches, community organizations, even television writers have a responsibility to contribute to the enterprise. We have a tendency to think that the schools should be able to take care of all our educational needs. But it doesn't work that way.

Not long ago *Parade* magazine asked teachers the question: What would help you do your job better? The most common answer was "students with a better attitude toward learning." The second was "more parental involvement with their children's education at home." Now, what do these two responses tell us? I think they tell us that when teachers walk into a classroom, they should be able to assume that there is a whole community of adults standing behind them. They should especially be able to assume that they have parents' support and help. It makes a big difference whether first-graders have been taught by parents not to interrupt and how to say thank you. It makes a big difference whether parents make sure their children do their homework, discuss school with them, visit their classrooms, and let them know how important education is.

If there is one thing I would ask, it is that teachers not be hesitant to send this message to their students' parents. Let parents know what is expected of them. Let them know it over and over again. Let them know that you're not asking for any favors—you're just letting them know what they're going to have to do if they want their children to have a good education. Call them, write them, meet with them, do whatever it takes. Sometimes, I know, it is frustrating. Sometimes you feel like you can't get any response. In my talks with teachers and principals all across this country, I've heard the same message over and over again: Get the parents involved, and everything else will fall into place.

These, then, are some of the things the American people expect of teachers, and some of the things they owe teachers. I remember reading something written by an American hero, Sam Houston. In his lifetime Sam Houston was a frontiersman, a soldier, a general, a U.S. senator, a governor, and even a president—president of the Republic of Texas. And for a while in Maryville, Tennessee, he was a teacher. Years later, as Sam Houston looked back over a lifetime of accomplishments, he wrote that being a teacher gave him a higher feeling of dignity and self-satisfaction than any other office or honor he had held.

There is still today something dignified and satisfying about teaching that no other profession can match—just as there was in Socrates' time, in Sam Houston's time, and in Sir Thomas More's time. I mention Thomas More because I'd like to end with a story about More as told by Robert Bolt in his play *A Man for All Seasons*. Bolt tells the story of a young man, Richard Rich, who approaches More for advice on prospective careers. Rich is a bright and ambitious young man and is considering law or politics. But instead Sir Thomas makes this suggestion to him: "Why not be a teacher?"

"You'd be a fine teacher. Perhaps even a great one," Sir Thomas adds.

"If I was," asks Rich, "who would know it?"

And Sir Thomas replies, "You, your pupils, your friends, and God. Not a bad public, that."

Indeed that isn't a bad public for teachers in this and in every age.

SIX

Heroes of the Republic *

IN TRAVELING EXTENSIVELY across the country, I repeatedly speak to educators and parents on what I believe matters most in education: the development of a child's intellect and character, and the relation of one to the other; providing our students with a foundation of shared knowledge; and the need for schools to transmit social and political values. In so doing, I have called on educators to do nothing less than commit themselves to what Plato thought to be a civilization's most important task: the upbringing, protection, and nurture of its children. These are solemn responsibilities. They deserve our serious and sustained attention.

Sometimes we as a society have given less than what is required; sometimes we have failed in our responsibilities. But there are grounds for hope. The tide has begun to turn. In the schools I have visited, I have seen firsthand how educators and parents have risen to the challenge, how they have placed themselves in the midst of the battle, for the sake of our children. And when I meet these people, when I witness the fruits of their labor, I thank them and pay tribute to them. They are, after all, real heroes of this republic.

* This chapter is based on an address delivered to the National Association for Vietnamese American Education, Arlington, Virginia, March 27, 1987.

Specifically I would like to pay tribute to Asian-Americans for the many lessons they have taught us all: lessons in education, and lessons, important lessons, about life. At this point let me insert a caveat. I know it is dangerous to generalize about any cultural group. And in the case of "Asian-Americans"—an umbrella term which covers more than twenty nationalities, and a far greater number of ethnic identities, each with its own language and culture—generalizations are particularly hazardous. Nevertheless, it seems to me that there are a number of qualities that reverberate throughout the Asian-American community that should concern us as educators: qualities that are noble and worthy of praise; qualities that make for a better society; qualities, therefore, that we must encourage and cultivate. I would like to elaborate on some of these qualities, particularly those that relate to education.

Of particular significance in educational performance is the existence of close ties between parents and children, and the willingness of parents to sacrifice for the sake of their children's education. At the Department of Education we have been saying for some time now that the parent is the child's most important teacher, the child's all but indispensable teacher.

There is by now a good deal of evidence, both statistical and anecdotal, that Asian-American children are outperforming their classmates. In an Asian-American community in Riverdale, New York, teachers and principals were puzzled that their textbooks were being sold at a rate faster, much faster, than the number of children registered in classes could account for. They wanted to know why. After doing a little investigating, they discovered that most Asian-American families were buying *two* sets of textbooks. One set was for the child, and a second set was for the mother, who could better coach her child if she worked during the day to keep up with his lessons. These teachers said that Asian-American children entering school in the fall with no English ability finished in the spring at the top of their classes in every subject. This is the kind of people, the kind of parents, who deserve honor.

Asian-American parents do not make these sacrifices simply so their children will do well materially. They do so out of a deep respect for learning. I am told that in Vietnam—when Vietnam was a free nation—teachers were revered. When Vietnamese are asked to describe their culture, "love of learning" is a character-istic frequently mentioned.

For most Vietnamese, this emphasis on learning has been maintained in the United States. A 1983 study by the Center for Applied Linguistics in Washington, D.C., noted that:

> The Vietnamese students' respect for teachers is a very no-ticeable characteristic in a typical American school, as it pro-motes behavior which is in contrast to that of some American students. The Vietnamese students, in general, are well-behaved, quiet and polite in the classroom, and some of our interviewees reported being horrified at some of the behaviors of their fellow classmates, such as talking back to teachers, telling a teacher to "shut up," talking in class, and putting their feet on a desk.

Yet another Asian-American quality that has a great deal to do with educational success is self-discipline, a willingness to do things the hard way, if that's what's required. A recent study prepared by Dr. Samuel Peng of the Department of Education demonstrated that Asian-American high school students spent considerably more time on homework, were less likely to be absent from school, and had higher educational aspirations than other students.

Finally, the experiences of many Asian-Americans were a bitter lesson in perseverance, industry, and courage. A three-year study of some 1,400 Indochinese households, conducted for the U. S. Office of Refugee Resettlement by Professor Nathan Caplan of the University of Michigan, concentrated on the most recent Indochinese refugees who risked their lives to escape the perse-cutions afflicting their homelands. Collectively, these refugees are often referred to in the press as the "boat people." Their escape was a truly fearsome and heroic ordeal. Adrift at sea, exposed to brutal pirate attacks and other cruel hardships, tens and perhaps hundreds of thousands of boat people never made it to safety. Today, they lie beneath the South China Sea—victims of Com-munist oppression and tyranny. Their fate serves as a reminder of the difference between freedom and totalitarianism. This con-flict is a moral conflict, of fundamental historical proportions, and gives the modern age its special meaning and peril. This is something those who have lived it can never forget. This is something the rest of us must never be allowed to forget.

Still, more than 730,000 Indochinese refugees made it to this nation, a nation they can now call home. The United States was proud to welcome them. The United States is proud to have them, as our newest immigrants, our newest citizens.

Unlike the more highly educated Vietnamese refugees who came here in the immediate aftermath of the fall of Saigon, the boat people had been farmers, fishermen, craftsmen, laborers, and students in Southeast Asia. Arriving with little or no knowledge of English, with no savings or other resources, and with few marketable skills, they faced seemingly insurmountable obstacles. "And yet," says Professor Caplan, "considering their hardships and all the odds against them, this group of immigrants has in fact demonstrated remarkable progress."

Nowhere has this progress been more remarkable than in the area of education. On national standardized tests of academic achievement, 27 percent of the refugee children scored in the 90th percentile on math achievement—almost three times better than the national average. And although they scored somewhat lower than the national average in English-language proficiency, they outperformed their peers on grade point average, with 27 percent earning A or A-minus. Overall, their scholastic average was 3.05 on a 4.0 scale, or slightly above a B. As Professor Caplan observed, a truly remarkable achievement. He writes, "The main reason for the success of these children appears to be due to the compatibility of what they bring with them—traditional cultural values, cohesive family structure, achievement orientation. . . . This may account for the rather rapid achievement of economic self-sufficiency by the parents, as well as the scholastic success of their children."

That study goes a long way toward explaining the success of these immigrants. Clearly, many fashionable theories about educational and social achievement—theories that emphasize the deterministic role of class, of the environment, of material factors, of "society"—do not apply here. On the contrary, what I believe the success of Asian-Americans demonstrates is the importance of *values*—values that people carry with them in their heads and in their hearts; values that remain with them when their possessions are gone and their homeland just a memory; values that sustain them for a lifetime.

Of course, the values that characterize the Asian-American community and account for its success—hard work, discipline, perseverance, industry, respect for family and for learning—are not confined to Asian-Americans alone. They are, in fact, traditional American virtues. They are virtues that were familiar to the Pilgrims, to readers of Benjamin Franklin's *Autobiography,* and to generations of American schoolchildren who learned from McGuffey's *Readers.* They are virtues preached down the ages by our greatest Americans. Let me recall the words of James Madison, "Father of the Constitution," in *Federalist* No. 55: "Republican government presupposes the existence of these qualities"—qualities of sound character and civic virtue—"in a higher degree than any other form."

The distinguished black American, Frederick Douglass said: "What we want . . . is character. . . . It is a thing we must get for ourselves. We must labor for it. It is gained by toil—hard toil. . . . It is attainable; but we must attain it, and attain it each for himself. I cannot for you, and you cannot for me."

Asian-Americans have reminded all of us of these fundamental truths; Asian-Americans have validated these time-honored beliefs, reminding us that they still work, that they will always work.

My admonition, my advice, is simple: As we strive for success in the future, let us first look to our past, to the values we share in common, and let us remain true to that past and to those values. And when we find success—individual success, group success, ethnic success—let us do our best to encourage imitation. Example, after all, is the language of men. We should look to those who speak it best.

There is one additional lesson we should learn from Asian-Americans, and it is this: A tremendous burst of creative energy is released when former victims of tyranny and oppression are presented with the very special opportunity that American society offers. For our free country offers the opportunity that Lincoln spoke of—an "open field and fair chance" for every American's "industry, enterprise, and intelligence." Our nation promises that we "may all have equal privileges in the race of life, with all its desirable human aspirations."

Many Americans take this promise for granted. Perhaps because so many Asian-Americans have personal experiences of the massive apparatus of repression by which Communist regimes hold their people in bondage, they may have a greater appreciation for the gift, the sacred gift, of freedom. And perhaps because of what they have endured to become citizens of this nation, they bring with them a determination to make the best use of the opportunities America offers.

Asian-Americans have put the rest of us in their debt. They have reminded us of both the opportunities and the responsibilities of American citizenship. And they continue to remind us, as Lincoln said, that a nation like ours "is worth fighting for, to secure such an inestimable jewel."

PART THREE

THE NURTURE AND PROTECTION OF OUR CHILDREN

SEVEN

The Family as Teacher *

THE FIRST BOOK of Kings tells us that when Solomon was king of Israel, two women came before him, each claiming to be the mother of the same infant. They asked for a judgment. Solomon ordered the child be cut in two and half the body be given to each woman. When, at this command, one of the women immediately gave up her claim, Solomon decreed that the child be given to her, because he knew then that she was the child's mother.

The truth that Solomon was counting on when he made his judgment is this: No one is more important to the nurture and protection of a child than a parent. As Solomon well knew, sensible government policy recognizes and takes advantage of this truth. Indeed, *sensible* government policy really has no choice where the welfare of a child is concerned, because seldom can a government match or replace the care a parent can offer.

When it comes to the education of our children, to the nurture and protection of our young, how have Americans as a whole been doing? During the 1960s and 1970s the American people put a lot of resources into improving the well-being of children. From 1960 to 1980, federal welfare spending rose 437 percent—from $69.2 billion to $302.8 billion. According to one report, by 1976

* This chapter is based on an address delivered to a Family Focus conference, Chicago, Illinois, November 11, 1986.

there were more than 260 federal programs in place with the sole or chief objective of helping children. During these same two decades, the amount of money spent per student on education each year has more than doubled. The average class size shrank, and the percentage of teachers with master's degrees rose from one-quarter to one-half.

How did children fare during those twenty years of unparalleled financial commitment? Regardless of the intentions of the social policies of the 1960s and 1970s, our children did not fare as well as we hoped they would. Here is a sample of the record during those twenty years, from 1960 to 1980; it is a different part of the record—not the money spent, but the outcomes:

- In our schools, SAT scores fell 85 points during those years.
- Births to unwed teenage girls rose 200 percent. The United States now has by far the highest rate of teenage pregnancy of any industrial nation—twice the rate of England, the closest competitor.
- In the seven years following the *Roe* v. *Wade* decision in 1973, the abortion rate for girls aged fifteen to nineteen nearly doubled. By 1980, nearly one-half of all teenage pregnancies ended in abortion.
- The rate of homicide among young people more than doubled from 1960 to 1980.
- Juvenile arrests more than doubled.

As for drugs, there is no way even to estimate the proliferation of drug use. Suffice it to say that when a 1986 *Weekly Reader* poll asked elementary school children what the most serious problem at school was, they said drugs. This is *Weekly Reader!* We are talking about *elementary school* children. And for teenagers, the use of PCP and cocaine, the most dangerous and most addictive drugs, is on the rise.

Some of these figures have improved since 1980, but the fact remains that no one can be satisfied when today's numbers are compared with the numbers of twenty-five years ago. My point here is not that our spending a lot of money caused this pathology. I am not saying that we should stop spending this money today. Nor am I saying that these hundreds of billions of dollars did not do some good. Of course they did. But it is clear that spending a lot of money certainly did not get our children to where we want them to be. It did not produce the effects we hoped for. That is a stubborn fact.

We must therefore look elsewhere for sources of our youth's problems. There is one source that is not difficult to locate, if we simply bear in mind the truth about the necessity of parents raising children, educating children, nurturing and protecting children. When children are having trouble, it is to the family that we should look first.

There is a problem with the American family—the traditional, so-called nuclear family. The problem lies with the diminishment of that family, for the biological, psychological, and educational well-being of our children depends on the well-being of families. As Michael Novak has written, the family is the original and most effective Department of Health, Education, and Welfare. If it fails to teach honesty, courage, desire for excellence, and a host of basic skills, it is exceedingly difficult for any other agency to make up for its failures.

In asserting this obvious truth, we do not deny that families may need expert help and advice at various points in the nurture and education of their children, particularly for children with special needs. We do not say that society is relieved of responsibility to do what it can when the family cannot do or is not doing its job. We do not mean that government entities or voluntary organizations should not try. They should. And they can sometimes do good, even great good. But society cannot replace the family. No matter how good the bureaucracy, it is not as good for a child as a good family.

The plight of the family has been much discussed in the media. It is by now well known to all. The research on this problem is clear: Take one of the parents permanently out of the home, and the educational health of the child is likely to suffer. Children from single-parent homes are more likely to have lower grades, more likely to be discipline problems in the classroom, more likely to skip school, to be expelled, and to end up as dropouts. They are more likely to experience emotional or psychological disturbance, to become involved with drugs, to get in trouble with the law.

This is not to say that a single parent cannot do a good job of raising children. Many do; they deserve our thanks and our praise. I have thanks and praise for one in particular: my mother, a divorced parent, who raised my brother and me. But it is obvious—it was obvious to me, and it was obvious to my mother—that it is much harder for one parent to raise a child than it is for two. This is another stubborn fact; it is simply a matter of having to spread oneself too thin.

The decline of the traditional American family constitutes perhaps the greatest long-term threat to our children's well-being. This country must not lose the most important educational institution of all, the one that has sustained and advanced our best ideals as a culture and as a civilization. This country must not lose the institution that has the unparalleled capacity to protect and nurture our children.

We hear much debate today about the roles of women in society, the responsibility of mothers toward children versus the demands of their careers. These questions are important, they need to be addressed. But I think they have overshadowed one that is equally important, and that question is this: *Where are the fathers?* I ask this because if you look at the breakup of the American family, you very quickly find that the fathers are the ones who are missing. Generally, the mothers are there struggling. For nine out of ten children in single-parent homes, the father is the one who isn't there. One-fifth of all American children live in homes without fathers. This is a fact which the public conscience is beginning to ponder. We are beginning to hear the question coming from many quarters: Where are the fathers? Where are the men? Wherever they are, this much is clear: too many are not with their children.

We know, then, where much of the research concerning youth and educational failure points: to the family. Regarding the causes of the family's struggles, we are much less certain. There are, no doubt, many pressures that have come to bear on the family in the last quarter-century. The web is extremely complex. But this much we can observe with certainty: the fabric of support which the American family could traditionally find in the culture at large has become worn, torn, and unraveled.

Our society is made up of a network of institutions, cultural beliefs, mores, and habits. That is to say, individuals live in environments in which certain ideas prevail, certain messages are sent. And these messages act to encourage or discourage particular attitudes and behaviors.

These messages ultimately greatly effect the existence and well-being of the family. It makes an enormous difference whether children get messages from television telling them that honesty is the best policy, and to honor their fathers and mothers—or whether they get messages telling them that adultery is the norm, and that the breakup of a family is an expected thing. Likewise, if schools, churches, elected officials, community institutions, and neighborhoods are reinforcing parents' efforts, it makes their jobs easier. If the institutions of society work at cross-purposes, the job is harder.

Everyone knows that a child needs and deserves a nurturing, sustaining environment. What is less commonly understood, but equally true, is that the *family* also needs and deserves a nurturing, sustaining environment. It is possible, of course, to think of the family as a refuge—a fortress against the outside world. But the family should not exist in such isolation. It needs a society reinforcing its efforts. The world around the family, the culture around the family, must give support. Too often today, it may do just the opposite. For example, there was a credo very popular in many schools during the sixties and seventies. It held that adults did not have the right to pass on traditional American values to children. Many children were taught this. It was an educational disaster, a pedagogical disaster, and a moral disaster. It helped to undermine the moral authority of the family.

We arrive, then, at the question of who or what can help the American family. The first answer, the unavoidable answer, is this: ultimately it is up to the efforts of individuals—individual mothers, individual fathers, individual families. Once again, it is a stubborn fact that will never go away. A family that has lost the conviction of its own irreplaceable mission, no outside agent can save. Other institutions—churches, schools, community organizations—should and must lend support. They can assist and guide. Above all, they must not stand in the way. But in the end, it is the commitment of individuals that counts: individual parents nurturing individual children.

This is not to absolve government of responsibility. Government—and in particular the federal government—has much to do here. Above all, I think, it is now the job of the federal government to help re-create the social fabric that used to give families support in raising children. This endeavor must happen in two stages.

First, public leadership must do what public leadership is supposed to do: lead. That leadership must affirm with no apologies the values and ideals which our tradition has affirmed as good. We must speak up for the family. We must say it loudly, and we must say it over and over again. Certainly, there is no shame, there is no second-class status, in raising a child by oneself. There is honor for those who can do it well. But we must say too that a husband and wife raising children together is preferable to a mother or father doing the job alone. It's better for the child, it's better for the parents. This is not something we can properly be neutral about.

I believe the federal government is well along the way in this first stage. President Reagan has consistently articulated to the nation the ideals of the family and family values. It is a hopeful sign that others in Washington are now talking seriously about the family, too. We need more. We need more elected officials, more political leaders, more community leaders to say it. We need more of those leaders who claim to speak for the poor and disadvantaged to say it. They need to speak up for the family as the pivotal redemptive institution for children. As Clifton Wharton has said:

> Recently, many of us have begun to ask again about the role of the family and the values embodied in families: discipline, hard work, ambition, self-sacrifice, patience, love. It is easy enough to mock such values as bourgeois. But middle-class or not, they increasingly appear to constitute the spiritual foundation for achievement.

The federal government is just entering the second stage of helping the family. Now that we are reaffirming these social values, we must look to see that social policies are in accord. We must make sure that federal policies are not doing things that weaken the fabric of the family. We must then look to see if state and federal policies can be restructured to give the family more incentive and support.

With respect to the field of education, it is my belief that any reform meant to help the family must follow two analogous stages. Again, it is ultimately up to individual effort—individual principals and teachers. But in general, schools must, first of all, be willing to teach respect and regard for the family as the bedrock institution of society. I do not mean that we should create courses on "parenting." Rather, schools must teach the value of the family and how it is the wellspring of a society's strengths. They must do this explicitly, through studies in history, literature, and civics.

Like the federal government, education too will have to go through a second stage of reform with respect to the family. Principals, teachers, school boards, and district and state officials must examine local policies. They must make sure those policies are doing nothing to alienate parents. And they must find strategies to pull parents back to the center of the educational process. This will mean reaching out to parents. It will mean giving them more say and more responsibility. We cannot restore our schools until we restore to them the truth that parents are the first, the fundamental, and, for most of us, the all but irreplaceable teachers. We will not have long-lasting educational improvement in this country without strong families.

There are reasons to be encouraged about the future health of the family. In general, I think that in the last five years the American people have had reason to feel better about themselves and their institutions. Several key indicators, such as the rates of divorce, violent crime, and youth suicide, have shown signs of bottoming out. SAT scores are rising again. The subject of the family—a subject often forgotten, ignored, and even disdained during the past two decades—is coming back into the limelight.

We have come upon a moment when the conditions of public concern are right for a turnaround. It would be tragic to lose that moment. But I do not think we will lose it if we can reaffirm the simple truth about needing the family. That is, I think the time and mood are such that the culture can begin to nourish families once again by sending encouraging messages. And that will happen when we *all* begin to speak up for the family. As Carolyn Wallace, who runs a community center in the heart of Newark, told journalist Bill Moyers in his report "The Vanishing Family":

> You gotta say it. . . . If you say it in your corner and I say it in my corner, and everybody is saying it, it's going to be like a drumbeat. And sooner or later it will sound. But it's not just for me to talk about, it's for all of us to talk about. . . . And you're not going to be safe, I'm not going to be safe . . . unless we all send out this drumbeat—hey, let's deal with it. Let's deal with the problem.

I agree. Let's deal with the problem. Let's do so by telling the truth, the truth about families and parents and children. In seeking the well-being of the children, we must look closely at the parents. This brings us back to the wisdom of Solomon, which brings us back to where I began.

EIGHT

Public Education and Moral Education*

I WOULD LIKE to begin with a story from ancient history, a very great story. It used to be familiar, but is remembered by too few today. It happened at a time when Rome was in great danger. The emperor Tarquin had been deposed and banished for his outrageous crimes, but he had gathered a massive Etruscan army and was pushing toward Rome in vengeful destruction. Villages were looted and the land pillaged. Finally, only the Tiber River remained between Rome and thirsty tyranny. And the Tiber could be crossed by only one wooden bridge.

Horatius was the guardian of the bridge. He saw the vast Etruscan army on the opposite bank, and he saw the frightened Romans behind him. He knew that time was short. "Give me two men," he told the Romans, "and we will hold the bridge on the far side long enough for you to break it down." And in a space wide enough for only three men to pass, Horatius and two others held an army at bay while their fellow citizens cut the bridge behind them. Those who have read the words of the English poet Thomas Macaulay are not likely to forget the deed:

•

* This chapter is based on an address delivered to the Eagle Forum Leadership Conference, Washington, D.C., September 21, 1985.

> *Then out spake brave Horatius,*
> *The captain of the gate:*
> *"To every man upon this earth*
> *Death cometh soon or late.*
> *And how can a man die better*
> *Than facing fearful odds*
> *For the ashes of his fathers*
> *And the temples of his gods."*

Now I would like to relate another story, an incident that happened not so long ago or far away. It happened to a substitute teacher in a suburban high school. He asked the students in his three advanced government classes what they saw as the most significant differences between the United States and the Soviet Union.

When it came to facts, he found that the students knew the Soviet record. They knew the truth about the Soviet Union. But he also found that they distrusted American institutions. And when he called for a show of hands, he found that only two out of fifty-three students felt that, despite our imperfections, the United States is a morally superior system to the Soviet Union. Put another way, fifty-one out of fifty-three of this affluent country's brightest high school seniors saw no moral difference between the United States and the Soviet Union.

I have to wonder what Horatius would say about such moral confusion. I wonder what he would say to the greatest nation on earth; a democracy that has attained gifts of political and individual freedom unequaled anywhere in any time; a country that raises some of its brightest children to regard the values of a totalitarian police state as morally commensurate with its own. I think Horatius would only ask a question: If this is how you raise your children, then when the time comes—and it will come, if the force of history has its way—who will be there to stand at your bridge?

Faced with institutions in which parents are no longer certain that solid values will be transmitted, many—those who can afford it, and many who struggle to afford it—have put their children in private schools. For many parents the nurture of values is at the heart of education, and these parents choose schools where values will be inculcated. I understand that kind of decision.

Parents have the responsibility to give their children the best education they possibly can, and we should help them in the exercise of that responsibility. But no matter what choice we make regarding our own children, none of us can abandon the effort to restore both intellectual and moral vitality to *public* education. Yes, I understand why parents may wish to walk away in frustration and anger from some schools. But for our children's sake there is a fight to be fought for our public schools, and it is a worthwhile fight. It is a fight that can be won, and I hope it is a fight that will be made.

Everything we know suggests that the vast majority of American children will, for the foreseeable future, go to public schools. None of those children should be relegated to a desert of moral relativism while others attend private institutions where solid values are taught. Why? Because the children in our public schools are our future teachers, statesmen, and corporate leaders. They are our future citizens, our future parents. Finding alternatives to public education where it is deficient is, in the end, not enough. Rather, we want the children in *all* of our schools to have the opportunity to learn the things we hold important. We want them to learn the values we cherish as a nation. We must care about our public schools; and we must care about the values taught in them.

I do not intend to impose a new demand on the principles that established public education. American public schools already have a time-honored tradition of instilling moral and democratic character. Our public school system did not spring forth all at once as the legislative child of congressional wisdom. It was put together piecemeal, over the course of several decades, community by community. Following the Revolutionary War, most early state constitutions expressed the common belief that education of the citizenry was necessary to domestic peace and prosperity as well as to individual morality. Schools existed in a hodge-podge of different forms. Students often attended private institutions run as businesses where teachers taught whatever parents paid to have taught. Churches, charities, and civic organizations, sometimes aided by government, often ran schools for poorer children. In the Northeast, so-called district schools emerged that were supported by local or state taxes.

Beginning in the mid-nineteenth century, a diverse, widespread group of crusaders began to work for public support of what was then called the "common school," the forerunner of the public school. The common schools were to be free, funded by local and state governments. They were to be controlled by local lay boards. And—this is important—they were to be charged with the mission of moral and civic training, training that found its roots in a ground of shared values. The advocates of the common school felt that the nation could fulfill its destiny only if every new generation was taught these values in a common institution.

The leaders of the common school movement were mainly citizens who were prominent in their communities—businessmen, ministers, civic officials. These people saw the common schools as upholders of standards of individual morality and a common denomination of civic virtues. The common schools were to be incubators of virtue, teaching moral messages even to very young students. For example, here is the final lesson, entitled "Goodby," from a book often used in the common school, McGuffey's *First Reader:*

> Now, my little readers, we have come to the end of the book, and I must bid you goodby. Before we part, let me give you a little advice.
>
> You are now a little child. You are but a few years old, and have not much wisdom. Therefore, always listen to your teacher and to your parents. They are older than you, and they know best what is for your good.
>
> Little children, you must love your parents. You should be kind to your teachers and gentle to your brothers and sisters, and playfellows. Use no hard words. Be guilty of no ill-natured tricks, and tell no ill-natured tales.
>
> Always do to other children as you wish them to do unto you. This is the "Golden Rule" — Remember it in your play. Act upon it now, and when you are grown up, do not forget it.

The common schools did not hesitate to be direct in teaching certain rules of good character. Today we would not agree with some aspects of the nineteenth-century vision for the public schools. Many common school promoters, for example, were intolerant of private and church-connected schools, which they mistakenly saw as harmful to progress and national unity. Others denounced orthodox religious belief as inherently divisive. Later, when Catholic immigrants arrived in our cities, many public school leaders believed that Protestantism was the American way and should be taught as such. Today we have left such prejudices behind and have widened our vision. But the important point is that the founders of the common schools had faith that public education could teach good moral and civic character from a common ground of American values.

Even with the coming of progressive education at the turn of the century, the understanding of the role of the public schools in forming character and fostering citizenship was not lost. But over the years it did begin to take a new form, and so did educational leadership. Like so many other groups in America, education leaders began to view themselves as a confederation of experts, sanctioned by training, tied together by professional associations, supported by science, and aided by elaborate research techniques. Their confidence in their own expertise became so optimistic, in fact, that one educator predicted that "through the knowledge of the science of human nature and its work in the industries, professions, and trades, the average graduate of Teachers College in 1950 ought to be able to give better advice to a high school boy about the choice of an occupation than Solomon, Socrates, and Benjamin Franklin all together could give."

They were indeed optimistic. Nevertheless, whatever the exaggerated claims of these men and women who considered themselves experts in education, they did not forget their role as teachers of character. At the turn of the century a leading urban educator told his colleagues that "it is left to you to be the only true superintendents, superintendents of a moral well-being." And in 1933 the yearbook of a major educators' association stated that the job of its members was nothing less than to "mold character and to ameliorate the whole intellectual, moral, social, civic, and economic status of their fellows."

In short, twentieth-century educational leaders saw as their role the teaching of many of the same values that an older generation had seen as the elements of good character and sound morality. But science and the notion of expertise gave their ambitions a new confidence, the confidence that they alone knew how to do it best. And the excessive belief in progress increasingly led these educators to leave "old-fashioned" values behind.

In the past quarter-century some of the so-called experts became proponents of value neutrality, and moral education seemed increasingly to have been left in their hands. The commonsense view of parents and the public, that schools should reinforce rather than undermine the values of home, family, and country, was increasingly rejected.

I believe that if the current reform movement is to succeed, it must rest on the conviction that the public schools belong to the public, not to the experts, or social scientists, or professionals, or the education establishment. Since becoming Secretary of Education I have met with many groups that profess to speak for the public schools. Several keep representatives or lobbyists in Washington. I have also spent a good deal of time traveling around the country, talking with individuals who care about our schools—parents, teachers, principals, businessmen. And I have noticed that what I hear in Washington, D.C., is often not in step with what I hear out there, in North Carolina or New Hampshire or Idaho or Louisiana, or in the schools of that very same Washington, D.C.

I have been criticized by some for listening too hard to the American people or, in other words, for not paying enough attention to the education establishment. For example, a September 1985 issue of a well-known education journal contains an editorial in its "Washington Report" section about what is labeled Bill Bennett's "ideological agenda." The editorial makes this complaint:

[A]n ideology that is out of touch with those who administer public education may get in the way. Bennett talks about his "Three C's"—content, character, and choice—but as he talks he looks past the leadership of public education. He brings his crusade to the American public, citing public opinion polls but overlooking the channels that must inevitably convey his message.

It is true, I have sometimes criticized and been criticized by members of the education establishment. But the education establishment is not the same thing as our public schools, and its members do not always speak either for or in the best interests of our public schools.

In many, many places our historic educational heritage is alive and well and doing an admirable job of bringing our children through the most important hours of their lives spent outside the home. I have returned renewed, and indeed inspired by what I found as I visited and taught in fine schools in such places as Shreveport, Louisiana, and Osburn, Idaho.

I am for the public schools and I respect their time-honored tasks. That makes me think all the more strongly that where some of them have come to fall short, we must do everything we can to improve them. I am for their coming home, and I shall work to that end, despite what some critics from the education establishment may say. And I shall continue to talk directly to the American people. In education it is high time we both talked to them and listened to them.

Our public schools once placed the building of character and moral discernment on a par with developing the intellect. And they can once again. We *can* get the values Americans share back into our classrooms. And we will work to do this. Those who claim we are now too diverse a nation, that we consist of too many competing convictions and interests to instill common values, are wrong. Yes, we are a diverse people. We have always been a diverse people. And as Madison wrote in *The Federalist*, the competing, balancing interests of a diverse people can help ensure the survival of liberty. But there are values that all American citizens share and that we should want all American students to know and freely to make their own: honesty, fairness, self-discipline, fidelity, love of country, and belief in the principles of liberty, equality, and the freedom to practice one's faith. The explicit teaching of these values is the legacy of the common school, and it is a legacy to which we must return.

Education shapes our future as a nation and as a people, and while some Americans will send their children to private schools, and should not be discouraged from doing so, most of our nation's children will attend public schools for their education. Our public schools deserve from us the very same thing James Madison said our country deserves from us: "loving criticism"—candor in the service of improvement, honest assessment toward the end of betterment.

There is no more important priority in education than the restoration of our public schools to a position of public respect and public confidence. With broad community and parental support, we can achieve this. We can have the schools that our children deserve. We can hold the bridge.

NINE

Moral Literacy and the Formation of Character *

THE TERM "values" may suggest that judgments of right and wrong, noble and base, just and unjust, are mere personal preferences, that things are worthwhile only if and insofar as individuals happen to "value" them. As a friend once said, when he hears the word "values" he reaches for his Sears catalog.

Rather than reach for a catalog, we need to reach for a new term. Because these issues are not matters of mere personal taste, let me propose that we reconsider the enterprise now known as "the teaching of values." Let me suggest that we relabel that enterprise as the effort to help form the character of the young and to aid them in achieving moral literacy. The formation of character and the achievement of moral literacy—that, I think, is what we really should be about.

Forming character must begin in the home, starting in the earliest childhood years, but after that, schools must help—because as President Eliot of Harvard once reminded us, "in the campaign for character no auxiliaries are to be refused." And the school can be a mighty auxiliary. There is fairly general agreement as to what elements constitute good character in an individual. You won't find many people who are going to argue: "No,

* This chapter is based on an address delivered to the Manhattan Institute, New York City, October 30, 1986.

honesty is not a part of good character," or "No, courage isn't really admirable." We all agree on the value of these things. Now, we may disagree on cases involving these traits, or when there are conflicts among competing claims, but we still maintain our allegiance to good character as a virtue, as something worth preferring.

But despite the beliefs of the majority of Americans, no sooner does anyone begin to point out how important it is to "teach values" in the schools than others immediately begin to raise the specter of awful complexity. As soon as someone starts talking about forming character at school, others claim that it just can't be done, that we won't find a consensus on what to teach or how to teach it. I have heard this complaint on and off, mostly on, in the fifteen years I've been writing on this issue.

A *New York Times* columnist recently wrote that if the people urging schools to teach values—including, he wrote, Governor Mario Cuomo and myself—were asked to define those values, they would probably find it hard to agree. And a *Washington Post* columnist, also writing about the Secretary of Education and the governor of New York, gave us this analysis: "In the United States, the most heterogeneous nation in the world, one man's values can be another man's anathema. . . . Does it really make any sense to add still further to [our schools'] burden, to insist that they provide the answers to questions of values upon which we mature adults cannot agree?"

And sometimes it is one and the same person who calls attention to the importance of teaching values and then immediately thinks better of his suggestion. So Governor Cuomo, talking about his plans to bolster the teaching of values in New York schools, immediately demurred: "You probably won't be able to get a consensus view on values, so it probably won't go anywhere, but we'll try."

Governor Cuomo is right to stress the importance of teaching values—but he shouldn't be so doubtful that it can be done. I agree there are hard cases. I agree there is not a consensus on everything. But nevertheless this task can be done, and should be done. It has been done for most of American history. While a certain amount of caution and prudence is of course healthy—no one wants to impose a moral straitjacket on children—we do not want to present them with a moral vacuum either. There is no reason for excessive timidity, in suggesting a role for our schools in the formation of character. In fact, there is an increasingly broad consensus today as to the importance of this task. My message is that it can be done, and that we should demystify this subject so we can get down to business.

The first mistake is to say that we cannot agree on "values." Well, we cannot agree on everything. But we can agree on the basic traits of character we want our children to have and that we want our schools to develop. And we can agree that there ought to be such a thing as moral literacy.

What do I mean by "moral literacy"? Professor E. D. Hirsch of the University of Virginia has pointed out that being literate entails more than recognizing the forms and sounds of words. It is also a matter of building up a body of knowledge enabling us to make sense of the facts, names, and allusions cited by an author. This background knowledge Hirsch calls cultural literacy. For example, someone who is unsure who Grant and Lee were may have a hard time understanding a paragraph about the Civil War, no matter how well he reads. Likewise, a reader who isn't familiar with the Bill of Rights will not fully understand a sentence containing the words "First Amendment." Understanding a subject, then, involves not just the possession of skills; it also depends on the amount of relevant prior knowledge a reader has, on his cultural literacy.

So it is with "moral literacy." If we want our children to possess the traits of character we most admire, we need to *teach* them what those traits are. They must learn to identify the forms and content of those traits. They must achieve at least a minimal level of moral literacy that will enable them to make sense of what they will see in life and, we may hope, will help them live it well.

So the question is: How does education form character and help students achieve moral literacy?

It seems that some have forgotten the answer. Some educators have turned to a whole range of mostly dubious "values education" theories, wherein the goal is to guide children in developing "their own values" by discussion, dialogue, and simulation. It is not unusual to hear educators say they should be neutral toward questions of right and wrong. I believe these views are mistaken.

For example, in 1985 the *New York Times* ran an article quoting New York area educators proclaiming that "they deliberately avoid trying to tell students what is ethically right and wrong." The article told of one counseling session involving fifteen high school juniors and seniors.

In the course of that session the students concluded that a fellow student had been foolish to return $1,000 she found in a purse at the school. According to the article, when the students asked the counselor's opinion, "He told them he believed the girl had done the right thing, but that, of course, he would not try to force his values on them. 'If I come from the position of what is right and what is wrong,' he explained, 'then I'm not their counselor.'" Now, once upon a time, a counselor offered counsel, and he knew that an adult does not form character in the young by taking a stance of neutrality toward questions of right and wrong or by merely offering "choices" or "options."

We would do well to remember that the Greek word *charakter* means "enduring marks," traits that can be formed in a person by an almost infinite number of influences. But as the theologian Martin Buber pointed out, the teacher is different from other influences in one important way: The educator is distinguished from all other influences "by his *will* to take part in the stamping of character and by his *consciousness* that he represents in the eyes of the growing person a certain *selection* of what is, the selection of what is 'right,' of what *should* be." It is in this will, Buber says, in this clear standing for something, that the "vocation as an educator finds its fundamental expression."

To put students in the presence of a morally mature adult who speaks honestly and candidly to them is essential to their moral growth. And it seems to me that this is why many teachers entered the profession in the first place—because they thought they could make a positive difference in the lives of students, in the development of their character, to make them better men and women.

We must have teachers and principals who not only state the difference between right and wrong, but who make an effort to live that difference in front of students. In this business of teaching character, there has never been anything as important as the quiet power of moral example. I once visited a class at Waterbury Elementary School in Waterbury, Vermont, and asked the students, "Is this a good school?" They answered, "Yes, this is a good school." I asked them, "Why is this a good school?" Among other things, one eight-year-old said, "The principal, Mr. Riegel, makes good rules and everyone obeys them." So I said, "Give me an example." And another answered, "You can't climb on the pipes in the bathroom. We don't climb on the pipes and the principal doesn't either."

This example is probably too simple to please a lot of people who want to make this topic difficult, but there is something profound in the answer of those children, something educators should pay more attention to. You can't expect children to take messages about rules or morality seriously unless they see adults taking those rules seriously in their day-to-day affairs. Certain things must be said and certain examples must be set—there is no other way. These are the first and most powerful steps in nurturing character and developing moral literacy in the young.

When it comes to instilling character and moral literacy in schoolchildren, there is of course the question of curriculum. What materials and texts should students be asked to read? The research shows that most "values education" exercises and separate courses in "moral reasoning" tend not to affect children's behavior; if anything, they may leave children morally adrift. So what kind of materials should we be using instead?

The simple answer is, we don't have to reinvent the wheel. And we don't have to add new courses. We have a wealth of material to draw on—material that virtually all schools once taught to students for the sake of shaping character. And it is subject matter that we can teach in our regular courses, in our English and history classes.

The vast majority of Americans share a respect for certain fundamental traits of character. Because they are not born with this knowledge, children need to learn what these traits are. They will learn them most profoundly by being in the presence of adults who exemplify them. But we can help their grasp and the appreciation of these traits through the curriculum. That is, we can invite our students to discern the moral of stories, of historical events, of famous lives.

Let me mention just a few examples. There are thousands.

Do we want our children to know what honesty means? Then we might teach them about Abe Lincoln walking three miles to return six cents and, conversely, about Aesop's shepherd boy who cried wolf.

Do we want our children to know what courage means? Then we might teach them about Joan of Arc, Horatius at the bridge, Harriet Tubman and the Underground Railroad.

Do we want them to know about kindness and compassion, and their opposites? Then they should read *A Christmas Carol* and *The Diary of Anne Frank* and, later on, *King Lear*.

Do we want them to know about loyalty to country? Then we should want them to know of Nathan Hale, about the Battle of Britain, and the siege at Thermopylae. They should know that men such as Lieutenant Elmo Zumwalt have served their country willingly, nobly. And they should understand the contrary examples of men like Benedict Arnold and John Walker.

We want our children to know what faithfulness to family and friends means, and so they should know how Penelope and Telemachus and even an old dog waited twenty years for Odysseus to come home. We want them to know about respect for the law, so they should understand why Socrates told Crito: No, I must submit to the decree of Athens.

We want them to know about persistence in the face of adversity, and so they should know about the Donner party, and the voyages of Columbus, and the character of Washington during the Revolution and Lincoln during the Civil War. And our youngest should be told about the Little Engine That Could.

We want our children to recognize greed, and so they should know King Midas. We want them to recognize vanity, and so they should read "Ozymandias" and learn about Achilles. We want them to know about overreaching ambition, so we should tell them about Lady Macbeth.

We want our children to know that hard work pays off, so we should teach them about the Wright brothers at Kitty Hawk and Booker T. Washington learning to read. We want them to see the dangers of an unreasoning conformity, so we should tell them about the Emperor's New Clothes and about Galileo. We want them to see that one individual's action can make all the difference, so we should tell them about Rosa Parks, and about Jonas Salk's discovery of a vaccine against polio.

We want our children to respect the rights of others, and so they should read the Declaration of Independence, the Bill of Rights, Gettysburg Address, and Martin Luther King, Jr.'s "Letter from Birmingham City Jail."

There are other stories we can include, too—stories from the Bible: Ruth's loyalty to Naomi, Joseph's forgiveness of his brothers, Jonathan's friendship with David, the Good Samaritan's kindness toward a stranger, Cain's treatment of his brother Abel, David's cleverness and courage in facing Goliath. These are great stories, and we should be able to use them in teaching character to our children. Why? Because they teach moral values we all share. And they shouldn't be thrown out just because they are in the Bible. As Harvard psychiatrist Robert Coles recently asked, "Are students really better off with the theories of psychologists than with the hard thoughts of Jeremiah and Jesus?" Knowing these hard thoughts is surely part of moral literacy, and it does not violate our Constitution.

These, then, are some of the familiar accounts of virtue and vice with which our children should be familiar. Do our children know these stories, these works? Unfortunately, many do not. They do not because in some places we are no longer teaching them. Why should we go to the trouble of picking up the task again? For several reasons.

First, these stories and others like them are interesting to children. Of course, the pedagogy will need to be varied according to students' level of comprehension, but you can't beat these stories when it comes to engaging the attention of a child. Nothing in recent years, on television or anywhere else, has improved on a good story that begins "Once upon a time . . ."

Second, these stories, unlike courses in "moral reasoning," give children some specific reference points. Our literature and history are a rich quarry of moral literacy. We should mine that quarry. Children must have at their disposal a stock of examples illustrating what we believe to be right and wrong, good and bad—examples illustrating that, in many instances, what is morally right and wrong can indeed be known.

Third, these stories help anchor our children in their culture, its history and traditions. They give children a mooring. This is necessary, because morality, of course, is inextricably bound both to the individual conscience and the memory of society. Our traditions reveal the ideals by which we wish to live our lives. We should teach these accounts of character to our children so that we may welcome them to a common world, and in that common world to the continuing task of preserving the principles, the ideals, and the notions of greatness we hold dear.

I have not mentioned issues like nuclear war, abortion, creationism, or euthanasia. This may come as a disappointment to some people, but the fact is that the formation of character in young people is educationally a different task from, and a prior task to, the discussion of the great, difficult controversies of the day. First things first. We should teach values the same way we teach other things: one step at a time. We should not use the fact that there are indeed many difficult and controversial moral questions as an argument against basic instruction in the subject. We do not argue against teaching physics because laser physics is difficult, against teaching biology or chemistry because gene splicing and cloning are complex and controversial, against teaching American history because there are heated disputes about the Founders' intent. Every field has its complexities and controversies. And every field has its basics.

So too with forming character and achieving moral literacy, or teaching values, if you will. You have to walk before you can run, and you ought to be able to run straight before you are asked to run an obstacle course. So the moral basics should be taught in school, in the early years. The tough issues can, if teachers and parents wish, be taken up later. And, I would add, a person who is morally literate will be immeasurably better equipped than a morally illiterate person to reach a reasoned and ethically defensible position on these tough issues. But the formation of character and the teaching of moral literacy come first, the tough issues later, in senior high school or college.

Further, the task of teaching moral literacy and forming character is not political in the usual meaning of the term. People of good character are not all going to come down on the same side of difficult political and social issues. Good people—people of character and moral literacy—can be conservative, and good people can be liberal; good people can be religious, and good people can be nonreligious. But we must not permit our disputes over thorny political or religious questions to suffocate the obligation we have to offer instruction to our young people in the area in which we have, as a society, reached a consensus: namely, on the importance of good character, and on some of its pervasive particulars.

I have spent much time as Secretary of Education traveling the country, visiting schools and teaching classes. I have taught seventh graders the Declaration of Independence, and eleventh-graders *Federalist* No. 10 and the story of the Constitutional Convention. To third-graders I've taught the story of Cincinnatus returning to his farm when he could have had an empire. And they got it. To the third-graders too, I've taught how nothing but George Washington's exemplary character stood against a mutinous army of unpaid soldiers bent on besieging the Continental Congress in Philadelphia, and how that shining character itself was enough to make those men turn back.

I have taught these lessons, and others, to American children. I have tried to teach them directly and unapologetically. I have talked to teachers and parents about these matters as well. And when I have very publicly done this in our classrooms, no one has ever stood up and said, "You shouldn't be teaching these lessons. You are indoctrinating our children, corrupting them, you are not respecting parental prerogative. This isn't the right stuff for our children to learn." On the contrary. People have been pleased. It has been my experience, in many trips across this country, that students and parents welcome such discussions; they want more, and most teachers and principals are not opposed to giving them more. There is a very broad, and very deep, consensus out there, and we are failing in our duty if we ignore it. Objections noted, cautions observed, let us get down to, and back to, the business of the moral education of the young.

TEN

Drug Use
Among Our Children*

MY CONCERN with student drug use began long before my arrival at the Department of Education—or even in Washington. That concern has deepened during my tenure as Secretary. In recent months, I have discussed this problem with parents and educators on visits to schools throughout the country. In addition, I have met with narcotics officers around the country to discuss the problem of school-age drug use.

How serious is our school-age drug problem? The best and most recent survey tells us that in 1985 sixty-one percent of all high school seniors—roughly two million young men and women—had tried illicit drugs. Forty-one percent had used drugs other than marijuana.

Most initial experiences with drugs now occur *before* high school. Almost one-third of the seventh graders in the State of New York, for example, reported that they had used illegal drugs before entering the seventh grade. In a 1983 poll, 25 percent of fourth graders reported pressure among their peers to try alcohol and marijuana. Among seventh graders, 50 percent reported pressure to try marijuana.

Now, some of these numbers—particularly those pertaining

* This chapter is based on testimony delivered before the House Committee on Education and Labor, Washington, D.C., August 6, 1986.

to regular marijuana use—are actually lower than they were in the late 1970's. But the levels of use remain unacceptably high, and the use of some drugs has gone up. Thirteen percent of high school seniors—the highest percentage ever—say they have used cocaine at least once in the last year.

Recently, a new, more powerful form of cocaine has become popular with some of the nation's young people in both the cities and suburbs. It's called crack. Crack is relatively inexpensive and is easier to use than cocaine. Its effect is quicker and more potent, and it may be the most addictive substance known. According to press accounts, some users report addiction after just one use. The use of PCP, or phencyclidine, is also on the rise in some areas. It's particularly popular among inner-city teens.

The facts on drugs are alarming. They're alarming to us, and they're alarming to our children as well. In 1985, when thirteen-to eighteen-year-olds were asked in a Gallup poll to identify the biggest problems confronting young people today, drugs topped their list. No other problem came close. In a second poll, four out of five high school students said that state laws regarding drug *dealing* are too lenient. And four out of five said that state laws regarding drug *use*—including marijuana use—are too lenient. Our children are seeking more forceful help from us.

Drug use concerns us all. And it's a special concern for our schools. Why? Let me offer three reasons. First, because students are taking drugs in our school buildings. Among 1985 high school seniors who said they had used cocaine in the last year, 22 percent reported using it in school. Forty-six percent of heavy drug users reported using marijuana in school within the last year.

Second, drug use undermines students' academic performance. Research tells us that students who use marijuana regularly are twice as likely as other students to average D's and F's. A study conducted in Philadelphia found that dropouts are twice as likely to be frequent drug users. I think the case here is clear: when students are using drugs, chances are they are not going to be learning.

Third, drugs can disrupt an entire school. When large numbers of students in a class are on drugs, or absent, the academic progress not just of the users, but of all those around them who have the good sense and courage to resist drugs, is retarded. And concentrated drug use brings to a school all those illegal activities whereby users support their habit.

So the question is, what do we do about student drug use?

School-based programs of drug prevention are relatively new, and evaluations of the programs are newer still. We are, however, getting an idea of what methods often do *not* work. We know that providing information is ineffective when the focus is on the effects of drug use occurring far in the future, and when the description of those effects is overblown. We also know that approaches that treat drug use as a response to emotional problems, and concentrate on treating those problems, are usually not very effective.

But there is hope. We are gaining an idea of the sorts of approaches that do work. Treating drug use as a social phenomenon—as a response to pro-drug messages given by peers, adults, and the media—shows considerable promise. This means that we must make sure that school authorities send a clear, unequivocal message to children that drugs are wrong and dangerous, and that they should be rejected. It means telling them of the short-term effects that come with drug use. And it means reinforcing student opinion against drug use. There is also evidence that the qualities conducive to drug-free schools are the qualities that characterize *good* schools. Among their common characteristics are strong leadership, schoolwide emphasis on basic skills, and high teacher expectations.

Parents must be actively involved. They must tell their children that the use of illegal drugs will not be tolerated, and they must enforce this lesson by the power of their own example. Parents must support educators and encourage them to take all necessary steps to get drugs out of our schools. Parents must also help each other by supervising children and seeing that healthy drug-free activities are available. And they should contact school personnel and other parents when they have reason to believe that children from other families are using drugs.

Communities are going to have to pull together. They are going to have to get tough. They must work with law enforcement officials and organize community agencies to ensure that schools have the support they need to fight drugs. It will not be easy. But where there are drugs, for the sake of the children, these things must be done. School boards can lead the way by setting tougher rules themselves. In the words of the *Washington Post,* school boards should give administrators "the best tool they could have: the ability to expel students involved in drug activity. Kick the pushers out of the schools."

What is the federal government's role in addressing the problem of student drug use? Clearly, we have a major part to play in the enforcement of laws governing drug use and drug sales. The government has a potent new weapon in the Comprehensive Crime Control Act of 1984, which makes it a federal crime to distribute a controlled substance within 1,000 feet of a school. In the summer of 1986, several Washington students, eighteen and nineteen years old, were indicted under the act. If convicted, they could serve up to thirty years in jail. "If they can sell drugs," says U.S. Attorney Joseph diGenova, "they can do the time." "To those who perceive these charges as heavy-handed," he added, "I suggest they go into the schools where teachers and principals are fighting to maintain civility."

In fiscal year 1986 the federal government will spend $1.7 billion to support anti-drug programs. These funds will be devoted to law enforcement efforts, prevention, medical treatment, and research. In addition, the federal government provides $300 million to state-administered alcohol and drug services. We at the Department of Education are working with the state and a number of federal agencies on the drug abuse problem.

Over the years, perhaps the most important role of the Department of Education has been to provide information: information on the condition of American education, and on which educational methods are effective and which are not. Early this year I asked my staff to initiate an intensive study of the available research on drug abuse in our schools and to determine the elements of effective prevention programs. In March I announced that a report to the American people, offering practical recommendations, based on the best available research, would be available in September. The book will be a follow-up to *What Works,* a guide to effective educational techniques that has proved remarkably popular.

Like *What Works,* our new book on preventing drug use, entitled *Schools Without Drugs* [published in September 1986], will be a straightforward, useful summary of the best information available on the subject.* Like *What Works*, it will be aimed not at other researchers or other bureaucrats, but at the nation's chief educational practitioners—parents, teachers, principals, and school administrators. It will be a handbook that they can understand, and that they can use—and that they can obtain free of charge. We think it will be a valuable guide in communities' assault on drugs.

I believe that drug prevention is a realm in which our dissemination of information can make a particularly important contribution. We need to get the word out. We need to tell the people in the trenches—the parents, teachers, principals, school boards, and religious and community groups—what works in preventing drug use.

* A free copy of *Schools Without Drugs* may be obtained by writing: Schools Without Drugs, Pueblo, CO 81009.

ELEVEN

Sex and the Education of Our Children *

I WOULD LIKE to discuss one place in which attention must be paid to character in an explicit, focused way. That is in the classroom devoted to sex education. It would be undesirable, but a teacher could conduct large portions of a class in English or history without explicit reference to questions of character. To neglect questions of character in a sex education class, however, would be a great and unforgivable error. Sex education has to do with how boys and girls, how men and women, treat each other and themselves—or, rather, *should* treat each other and themselves. Sex education is therefore about character and the formation of character. A sex education course in which issues of right and wrong do not occupy center stage is evasive and irresponsible.

Sex education is much in the news. Many localities are considering proposals to implement or expand sex education curricula. I understand the reasons why such proposals are under consideration. And indeed, polls suggest that a substantial majority of the American people favor sex education in the schools. I too tend to support the idea. It seems altogether reasonable for the schools to provide another opportunity for students to become both more knowledgeable and more thoughtful about this im-

* This chapter is based on an address delivered to the National School Boards Association, Washington, D.C., January 22, 1987.

portant area of life. To have such matters taught by adults whom students and their parents trust would be a great improvement on the sex curriculum available on the street and on television.

For several years now, though, I have been looking at the actual form sex education assumes once it is in the classroom. Having surveyed samples of the literature available to the schools, and having gained a sense of the attitudes that pervade some of this literature, I must say this: I have my doubts. It is clear to me that some programs of sex education are not constructive. In fact, they may be just the opposite. Some schools, to be sure, are doing an admirable job. But in all too many places, sex education classes are failing to give the American people what they are entitled to expect for their children, and what their children deserve.

In 1985, 70 percent of all high school seniors had taken sex education courses, up from 60 percent in 1976. Yet when we look at what is happening in the sexual lives of American students, we can only conclude that it is doubtful that sex education is doing much good. The statistics are little short of staggering:

- More than one-half of all adolescents have had sexual intercourse by the time they are seventeen.
- More than one million teenage girls become pregnant each year. Of those who give birth, nearly half are under eighteen.
- Teen pregnancy rates are at or near an all-time high. A 25 percent decline in birth rates between 1970 and 1984 is due to a doubling of the abortion rate during that period. More than 400,000 teenage girls now have abortions each year.
- Births among unwed teenage girls rose 200 percent between 1960 and 1980.
- Forty percent of today's fourteen-year-old girls will become pregnant by the time they are nineteen.

These numbers are an irrefutable indictment of sex education's effectiveness in reducing teenage sexual activity and pregnancies. For these numbers have grown even as sex education has expanded. I do not suggest that sex education has *caused* the increase in sexual activity among youth; but clearly it has not prevented it. As Larry Cuban, professor of education at Stanford University, has written, "Decade after decade . . . statistics have demonstrated the ineffectiveness of such courses in reducing sexual activity, unwanted pregnancies, and venereal disease among teenagers. . . . In the arsenal of weapons to combat teenage pregnancy, school-based programs are but a bent arrow. However, bent arrows do offer the illusion of action."

Why do many sex education courses offer merely the illusion of action? When one examines the literature and materials available to the schools, one often discovers in them a certain pervasive tone, a certain attitude. That attitude is this: Offer students technical information, offer the facts, tell them they have choices, and tell them what the consequences of those choices could be, *but do no more*. And therein is the problem.

Let me give a few examples. And let me say that these are not "worst case" examples—that is, they are not samples of the most controversial and provocative material used in sex education courses. They are, rather, approaches commonly used in many schools.

A curriculum guide for one of the largest school systems in the country suggests strategies to help "students learn about their own attitudes and behaviors and find new ways of dealing with problems." For example, students are given the following "problem situation," asked to "improvise dialogue" and "act out" the problem, and then discuss "how everyone felt about the interactions."

> Susan and Jim are married. He becomes intoxicated and has sex with his secretary. He contracts herpes, but fails to tell Susan. What will happen in this situation? How would you react if you were Susan and found out?

The "expected outcome" of this exercise in "acting out" and "interacting" is to get the student "to recognize sexually transmitted diseases as a threat to the health of the individual."

Another lesson presents a situation of an unmarried girl who has become pregnant. Various people in her life recommend various courses of action—from marriage to adoption to abortion. Having described the situation, the teacher is then supposed to ask the following questions:

Which solution do you like best? Why?
Which solution do you like least? Why?
What would you do if you were in this situation?

And the "expected outcome" of this exercise is "to identify alternative actions for an unintended pregnancy." Now, we know what
will likely happen in the classroom discussion of this lesson. Someone will opt for one course of action, others will argue for something else, more will speak, the teacher will listen to all opinions,
and that will be that. The teacher will move on, perhaps saying
the discussion was good—that students should be talking about
this. As though by talking about it, even if they do not arrive at
a clear position, they are somehow being educated.

Exercises like these deal with very complex, sensitive, and
often agitated situations which involve human beings at their
deepest levels. But the instruction to teachers in approaching all
such "sensitive and personal issues" is this, and I quote: "Where
strong differences of opinion exist on what is right or wrong sexual behavior, objective, informed and dignified discussion of both
sides of such questions should be encouraged." And that's it—
no more. The curriculum guide is loaded with devices to help
students "explore the options," "evaluate the choices involved,"
"identify alternative actions," and "examine their own values." It
provides some facts for students, some definitions, lots of "options"—but that's all.

What's wrong with this kind of teaching? First, it is a very
odd kind of teaching—very odd because it does not teach. It does
not teach because, while speaking to a very important aspect of
human life, it displays a conscious aversion to making moral distinctions. Indeed, it insists on holding them in abeyance. The
words of morality, of a rational, mature morality, seem to have
been banished from this sort of sex education. It is tantamount to
throwing up our hands and saying to our young people, "We give
up. We give up on teaching right and wrong to you. Here, take
these facts, take this information, and take your feelings, your
options, and try to make the best decisions you can. But you're
on your own. We can say no more." It is ironic that in the part
of their lives where children may most need adult guidance, and

where indeed, I believe, they most want it, too often the young find instead an abdication of responsible moral authority.

Now I ask this: Do we or do we not think that sex for children is serious business, entailing serious consequences? If we do, then we cannot be neutral about it. When adults maintain a studiously value-neutral stance, the impression likely to be left is that, in the words of one twelfth-grader, "No one says not to do it, and by default they're condoning it." And a sex education curriculum that simply provides options, and condones by default, is giving the wrong message.

It is not that the materials used in most of our schools are urging students to go out and have sexual intercourse. In fact, they give reasons why students might want to choose not to have intercourse, and they try to make students "comfortable" with that decision. Indeed, you sometimes get the feeling that, according to these guides, being "comfortable" with one's decision, with exercising one's "option," is the sum and substance of the responsible life. Decisions aren't right or wrong, decisions simply make you comfortable or uncomfortable. It is as though "comfort" alone has now become our moral compass. These materials are silent as to any other moral standards, any other standards of right and wrong by which a student might reach a decision to refrain from sex and which would give him or her the inner resources to stick by it.

We should not wonder, then, at the failure of sex education to stem the rising incidence of teenage sex, teenage pregnancies, teenage abortions, and single teenage parents. One developer of a sex education curriculum admits, "If you measure success in terms of reduction of teen pregnancy, I don't know if it has been successful. But in terms of orientation and preparation for students to comfortably incorporate sexuality into their lives, it has been helpful." There's that telltale "comfortable" again. I think most parents want to urge not what might be the "comfortable" thing, but the right thing. Why are we so afraid to say what that is?

The American people expect from sex education courses in the schools that their children will be taught the basic information, the relevant biology, the relevant physiology—what used to be called the "facts of life." But they also expect that those facts will be placed in a moral context. In a recent national poll, 70 percent of the adults surveyed said they thought sex education programs should teach moral values, and about the same percentage believed the programs should urge students not to have sexual intercourse. And, believe it or not, that adult consensus is actually paralleled by young people who take sex education courses. According to a recent survey, seventh- and eighth-graders say that the single greatest influence on their decision whether or not to engage in intercourse is the fact that "it is against my values for me to have sex while I am a teenager." Social science researchers report that factual "knowledge alone has little impact, and that even peer pressure is less powerful than the student's internalized beliefs and values."

How, then, might sex education do better in shaping the beliefs and values of our children? It could do better by underpinning the whole enterprise with frank attention to the *real* issue, which has to do with responsibility for oneself and for one's actions. This means explaining and defending moral standards in sexual behavior and offering explicit moral guidance. For example, why not say in schools exactly what most American parents say at home: children should not engage in sexual intercourse. Won't our children better understand such a message, and internalize it, if we say it to them in school as well as at home? Why *isn't* this message being taught in more classrooms?

In general, there seem to be three excuses put forth as to why the schools do not teach such lessons in character. First, it is said that, given the diversity of today's society, you could never determine whose values to put into the sex education curriculum, and you should not indoctrinate the young with your beliefs or anyone else's. (Apparently being "comfortable" with one's decision is the only consensual value left.)

I cannot buy this reasoning because it seems to me that when it comes to the well-being of our children, there are certain precepts to which virtually all Americans adhere. For example, I have never had a parent tell me that he or she would be offended by a teacher telling a class that it is better to postpone sex. Or that marriage is the best setting for sex, and in which to have and raise children. On the contrary, my impression is that the overwhelming majority of parents would gratefully welcome help in transmitting such values. And I don't think they would view this as indoctrination. It is simply ethical candor. To put students in the presence of a mature adult who speaks honestly and candidly to them is not to violate their rights or to fail to respect their diversity.

Second, it is said that teenage sex is so pervasive now that we should simply face reality and surrender any quaint moral notions we continue to harbor about it. The kids are going to have sex no matter what, so we ought to head off pregnancies by making sure they have contraceptives. As a member of one Washington lobbying organization said recently, "All of us wish teenagers wouldn't have sex, but Reagan and Bennett are dealing with the world as they would like it and we're looking at it as it is."

Well, Reagan and Bennett *are* talking about the world as it is, and I would like to assert that it violates everything a school stands for simply to throw in the towel and say, "Okay, we give up. It's not right, but we can't seem to do anything about it, so we're not going to worry about it any more." Yes, sex entices from many parts of the culture. So does violence. So do drugs. But school is supposed to be better, and do better, and point to a better way. After all, we can accept reality while also trying to shape it and improve it. If school were no better than TV, parents would just leave their children to sit at home and watch the tube all day long. School is supposed to be better. Parents who are trying to do right by their children, who are trying to shape their children's character, need an ally in the schools. They do not need another opponent or, almost as bad, an unprotesting "option" provider. And furthermore, not "everybody" is doing it, and we might wish to give those youngsters—half of our seventeen-year-olds—support and reinforcement, too.

There is simply no reason to assume that efforts to shape character in matters of sex are doomed to failure. In fact, there are encouraging signs to the contrary. A teen services program at Atlanta's Grady Memorial Hospital, for example, found that of the girls under age sixteen it surveyed, nine out of ten wanted to learn how to say no. Let me underline this. This is not Reagan and Bennett talking, it's girls under sixteen talking. Well, one way to help them say no is for adults to teach them the reasons to say no, and to give them the necessary moral support and encouragement to keep on saying it.

The third excuse for giving up on the teaching of character in sex education was stated most recently by a panel of scientific experts. The much-publicized report on teenage pregnancy by the National Research Council of the National Academy of Sciences draws one conclusion that few, I think, would disagree with: sexual activity among teenagers is intimately connected with self-image. As the report states, "Several studies of social and psychological factors associated with adolescents' sexual behavior conclude that self-perception (not self-esteem)—that is, the sense of what and who one is, can be, and wants to be—is at the heart of teenagers' sexual decision making."

This would be a good starting point for any educational project aimed at helping adolescents understand ways in which premature sex hinders the possibilities of becoming who they can be, who they want to be. But, strangely enough, the National Research Council reverses course, saying, "We currently know very little about how to effectively discourage unmarried teenagers from initiating intercourse." Rather than drawing a conclusion from the studies on self-perception, the Council simply accepts the inevitability of teenage sexual activity and urges "making contraceptive methods available and accessible to those who are sexually active and encouraging them to diligently use these methods [as] the surest strategy for pregnancy prevention."

I have a couple of observations about this. One, there is no evidence that making contraceptive methods more available is the surest strategy for preventing pregnancy—to say nothing about preventing sexual activity. Nor is it true that we know very little about how to discourage teenagers from sexual activity. It is true that what we know about such matters is not easily amenable to being measured and quantified. Nevertheless, we do know how to develop character and reinforce good values. We've known for quite a long time. As columnist William Raspberry has said, you do it the old-fashioned way. You make it clear to young people that there are moral considerations in life. You make it clear through habit, example, precept, and the inculcation of standards. This is not only possible, it has been tested and proven through centuries of experience. It seems to me that the National Research Council is acting with an extravagantly single-minded blindness when it simply, in the name of science, ignores such experience and offers instead a highly mechanical and bureaucratic solution—more widely available contraceptives in the schools.

The National Research Council's solution betrays a view of sex—and of life—that is dangerous for our children. For to suggest to teenagers that really the only thing that matters in sexual activity is guarding against pregnancy or sexually transmitted diseases—to suggest that the act of sexual intimacy is not significant in other ways—is to offer them still another very bad lesson. Why? Because it's false. It's false because, as every adult knows, sex is inextricably connected to the psyche, to the soul, or, if you don't like that term, to personality at its deepest levels. It is no mere riot of the glands that occurs and then is over and meaningless thereafter. Sexual intimacy changes things—it affects feelings, attitudes, one's self-image, one's view of another. Sexual activity takes place within the context of what is brought to it or left out of it by persons who engage in it. It involves men and women in all their complexity—their emotions, desires, and the often contradictory intentions that they bring with them, whether they mean to or not. It is, in other words, a quintessentially moral activity.

All societies have known this and have taken pains to regulate sexual activity. All societies have done so, sometimes wisely, sometimes not, because they have recognized that sex is fraught with mystery and passion, involving the person at the deepest level of being. As John Donne wrote, "Love's mysteries in souls do grow." Poets and philosophers, saints and psychiatrists have known that the power and beauty of sex lie precisely in the fact that it is *not* like anything else, that it is not just something you like to do or don't like to do. Far from being value-neutral, sex may be the most value-loaded of any human activity. It does no good to try to sanitize or deny or ignore this truth. The act of sex has complicated and profound repercussions. And if we're going to deal with it in school, we'd better know this and acknowledge it. Otherwise, we should not let our schools have anything to do with it.

Our children, too, have to know this. To deny the importance of sex, making it out to be something less special and powerful than it is, is a dodge and a lie. And it is just as much a dodge to silence a child who is awakening to an interest in sex. We serve children neither by denying their sexuality nor by making it a thing of no moral account.

I would like to offer a few principles that speak to the task of educating children about sex, principles which I believe should inform curricular materials and textbooks, and by which such materials could be evaluated. These principles are, I believe, what most American parents are looking for in sex education.

First, we should recognize that sexual behavior is a matter of character and personality, and that we cannot be value-neutral about it. Neutrality only confuses children, and may lead them to erroneous conclusions. Specifically, sex education courses should teach children sexual restraint as a standard to uphold and follow.

Second, in teaching restraint, courses should stress that sex is not simply a physical or mechanical act. We should explain to children that sex is tied to the deepest recesses of the personality. We must tell the truth; we must describe reality. We should explain that sex involves complicated feelings and emotions. Some of these are ennobling, and some of them—let us be truthful—can be cheapening of one's own finer impulses and cheapening to others.

Third, sex education courses should speak up for the institution of the family. To the extent possible, courses should speak of sexual activity in the context of the institution of marriage. They should stress the fidelity, commitment, and maturity required of the partners in a successful marriage.

To the girls, teachers need to talk about the readiness for motherhood. And they must do more. They must not be afraid to use words like "modesty" and "chastity." Teachers and curriculum planners must be sure that sex education courses do not undermine the values and beliefs that still lead most girls to see sexual modesty as a good thing. For it is a good thing, and a good word. Let us from time to time praise modesty. And teachers must not be afraid to teach lessons other girls have learned from bitter experience. They should quote Lani Thompson, from T. C. Williams High School in Alexandria, Virginia, who says of some of her friends: "I get upset when I see my friends losing their virginity to some guy they've just met. Later, after the guy's dumped them, they come to me and say, 'I wish I hadn't done it.' "

And the boys need to hear these things, too. Teachers should tell the boys what it is to be a father, what the responsibilities of being a father are. And they should tell them how the readiness for and responsibility of being a father should precede the acts which might make them fathers.

Fourth, sex education courses should engage parents as allies. Parents should be welcome in sex education classrooms as observers. If they are not, I would be suspicious. Parents should be informed of the content of these courses and encouraged to talk to their children about sex. Studies show that when parents are the main source of sex education, children are less likely to engage in sex. This should come as no surprise when one remembers that the home is the crucible of character, and that parents are children's first and foremost teachers.

Many parents admit that they do not do enough to teach their children about sex. But still, parents, more than anyone else, make the difference. Sex education courses can help remind parents of their responsibilities. And these courses should encourage the individual counsel of priests, ministers, rabbis, and other adults who know a child well and who will take the time and offer the advice needed for that particular child. For it is the quality of the care and time that adults take with children that means the most in the formation of character.

Finally, parents should pay attention to who is teaching their children about sex. They should remember that teachers are role models for young people. And so it is crucial that sex education teachers offer examples of good character by the way they act, and by the ideals and convictions they articulate to students.

These, then, are some of the principles I would like to see standing behind our schools' sex education courses. Part of the parents' job is to help inform the philosophies that guide their children's schools. Above all else, I would urge parents to make sure the schools are teaching their children the truth. Sometimes the simplest way to recognize the truth is to consult common sense, and never mind the pronouncements of so-called sex-ed experts. Character education is mostly a matter of common sense.

If sex education courses are prepared to deal with the truth, with reality in all its complexity, with the hard truths of the human condition, then they should be welcome in our schools. But if sex education courses are not prepared to tell the truth, if instead they want to simplify or distort or omit certain aspects of these realities in this very important realm of human life, then we should put them out of business. If sex education courses do not help in the effort to provide an education in character, then let them be gone from the presence of our children.

TWELVE

AIDS: Education and Public Policy *

ADULTS MUST DO everything we can to guarantee the health of our children, to protect them from the threat of disease. We must do all we can to see to it that they grow up in an environment that is not threatening to their basic well-being. And we have an obligation to do our utmost to pass on to them a society that is sounder economically, socially, and spiritually than the one we inherited. Acquired Immune Deficiency Syndrome (AIDS) is a threat to us, and to our ability to fulfill this obligation to our children. These are important reasons for concerning ourselves with AIDS.

First, let me state my views on educating our children about AIDS. Our young people deserve the best scientific and medical information about this disease, and about the ways in which it is transmitted. On this point, there is no argument. The federal government has an obligation, a duty, to provide this information to local education authorities. In schools that teach sex education, such courses should include a discussion of what is known about AIDS and the threat it poses.

Second, decisions on how we should teach the subject of

* This chapter is based on an address delivered at Georgetown University in April 1987 and adapted for the *Saint Louis University Public Law Review*, Vol. 7, No. 1 (1988).

AIDS—the proper timing of instruction, the particular content of instruction, and the like—are fundamentally ones for local communities to make. As with sex education courses in general, it is especially important in a sensitive area like AIDS education that school officials consult with parents, local public health officials, and community members to determine when and how to introduce such material into the classroom.

Third, the young people in our schools must be told the truth—that the best way to avoid AIDS is to refrain from sexual intercourse until, as adults, they are ready to establish a mutually faithful, monogamous relationship.

This issue—encouraging sexual abstinence among the young and sexual fidelity as the norm—has generated a lot of controversy. My own position has been caricatured as both out of touch and behind the times, and I have been accused of advocating methods that apply, if at all, to another age. Now, I may be a lot of things, but I do not think that I am either out of touch or behind the times.

In the first place, neither I nor anyone in the Reagan administration views sexual abstinence and fidelity as if they were the *only* means of combatting the AIDS epidemic. No one in this administration is arguing that we restrict our efforts to counseling abstinence or fidelity. In fact, abstinence and fidelity are being presented in conjunction with—not in lieu of—many other efforts.

These efforts are making progress. In just a few years, the disease has been identified and its characteristics delineated; epidemiological studies have been undertaken; the causative virus has been isolated; a blood test for the AIDS antibody has been developed; treatment agents have been developed; and preliminary work on a vaccine has been initiated. And there has been a rapid expansion of funding for research, treatment, and prevention of the disease.

I've never argued that we should simply preach sexual abstinence without explaining to students the whys and wherefores of the argument. Indeed, with regard to sex education, it isn't enough to tell kids just to say no. Given the culture in which our children grow up, saying no requires them to draw upon reserves of moral stamina that it is up to us, the adults, to instill in them.

We need to do more than preach at them. And I think adults can do more.

Urging abstinence is not simply a matter of shaking one's finger at children. You don't talk to young people about sexuality either by denying that they are sexual beings or by asking them to deny their own obvious interest in sexuality. We need to give children good reasons, fortifying reasons, for saying no. Some of these reasons will, in the nature of the case, be negative in character. AIDS is one such reason, and a powerful one. Preventing pregnancy is another. Not getting involved in situations beyond their emotional and psychological capacities is still another.

But if we can talk to the young about the physical and psychological dangers of sexual promiscuity, we can also talk about the positive reasons for self-control. These reasons have to do with the formation of character; with the value an individual places on his or herself, and larger purposes of his or her life; with our commitment to that bedrock institution of society, the family. We can talk about all these values, and we can honestly and forthrightly point to self-control as the positive route to their achievement. Restraint, in short, does not mean denying one's sexuality. It means mastering it. It means educating it. Is such an education desirable? Yes, it is. Is it possible? Yes, it is.

Now, to critics who say that, instead of talking mostly about sexual abstinence or fidelity, we should be talking about condoms, clinics, and clean needles, let me respond: the facts are otherwise. The facts are that abstinence and fidelity are the best means of guarding against AIDS that we currently know; there are none better. As President Reagan has said, "When it comes to preventing AIDS, don't medicine and morality teach the same thing?" Research findings tells us that the answer to that question is, "Yes, they do."

Look at the argument for abstinence and fidelity from a strictly utilitarian point of view—from a value-free perspective—and you will still arrive at the same conclusion: abstinence and fidelity are our best options. Abstinence and fidelity save lives. To ignore that fact—to refrain from telling it to our children—would be irresponsible.

Many others, by the way, have been making these points. Dr. John J. Coury, Jr., president of the American Medical Association, said, "If people out there are having multiple sexual experiences and going to houses of prostitution, they're playing Russian roulette. What we're talking about is preventing death." Surgeon General C. Everett Koop called sexual abstinence among young people and monogamy among adults the best measures to defeat the AIDS epidemic. "If you have a monogamous relationship, keep it," he said. "If you don't have one, get it." Floretta McKenzie, school superintendent in Washington, D.C., told teachers that they should not only warn their students about the perils of sex at a young age but advise them to abstain from sexual activity.

The case for sexual abstinence or fidelity, then, is in part a case for taking AIDS seriously. If parents want to counsel the use of condoms, or authorize others to do so, that is fine; but to rely excessively on condoms as a solution—what I have called "condom-mania"—is an evasion. It is at best a half-measure. Condoms are not 100 percent reliable, and their prospective users are not 100 percent reliable either. At worst, excessive reliance on condoms is self-delusion. Indeed, in dealing with AIDS in general, I wonder if we haven't been guilty of a number of such half-measures and evasions, and especially of evading a real debate about the hard choices that now face us.

To help encourage such a debate, I would like to make a few suggestions that could help inform our public deliberations on AIDS. There are, I think, certain fundamental goals that we can all agree on. The difficulty, the challenge, lies in deciding the means for achieving these goals, and the proper balance between competing principles and considerations. It is on these points that we need to engage in a robust public debate.

One goal that we all seek is to find a cure for AIDS. This means, among other things, funding intensive research, exploring more effective ways to coordinate government and private efforts, and doing what we can to assist the scientific community in finding a cure.

A second goal we all endorse is to care for those afflicted with AIDS. We as a society have an obligation to minister to the sick and suffering in our midst. We must, accordingly, do what is necessary to ensure that families, social services, and health care facilities have the resources to provide adequate medical care and support for those suffering from this disease.

And we must oppose, firmly and unambiguously, any discrimination against those who have contracted AIDS. We must prevent the persecution, through ignorance or malice, of our fellow citizens. That is simply not acceptable, not in America, not today.

We should also help eradicate false fears which surround AIDS. We have, in fact, been doing quite a good job of this. And we must make it as easy as possible for those who are afflicted with the virus to seek help; this means, among other things, ensuring that our testing capabilities are sufficient so that individuals can discover if they are carriers of the virus, and can receive appropriate counseling and care.

Finally, a third goal on which we all agree—protecting the public health. We have as solemn a responsibility to protect the uninfected as we do to care for the afflicted.

Already AIDS has spread from its primary risk groups, homosexuals and intravenous drug users, to heterosexuals; now it is attacking the newborn as well. It is estimated that by 1991, four thousand new babies will have contracted AIDS from being exposed to the virus while in the womb. Furthermore, as the disease spreads, children will become increasingly at risk. This danger to our children makes it all the more urgent that we do everything in our power to protect society.

One way to protect the public is by the right kind of education. We need to instruct people about how to protect themselves from AIDS, and how to distinguish false fears from real fears. A second way is by stating clearly the obligation of those who are infected, or who have reason to think they may be infected. We all have a moral obligation not to endanger others. And so, we need to say this: If you have reason to believe you may be a carrier of the AIDS virus, you have an obligation to undergo AIDS testing. And if you are found to be a carrier of AIDS, you have an obligation to refrain from any activity that will endanger the health of another person.

This, it seems to me, is a basic social and individual responsibility. And we shouldn't be afraid to say publicly and repeatedly that those who don't meet that responsibility—those who endanger the lives of others because they choose to remain ignorant or to behave recklessly—are behaving wrongly. Ignorance cannot be used to justify irresponsible, life-threatening social behavior. As Willard Gaylin, president of the Hastings Center, wrote in the *New York Times,* "A person who is at risk and refuses to have himself tested must behave as though he had been tested and found positive. To do otherwise is cowardice compounding hypocrisy with wrongdoing."

Finally, I think we need to ask some hard questions and debate some of the hard choices surrounding AIDS—questions like whether routine testing might be advisable under certain circumstances, whether "contact notification" might not be necessary, and whether spouses or lovers have a right to be informed if their partner is found to be infected with AIDS.

The Surgeon General, as well as a number of public health professionals, has called for expanded testing. Testing is necessary to track the spread of the disease and to determine the effectiveness of measures taken to combat it. Testing is also necessary to identify those who are infected, so they can act in ways that will reduce the likelihood that they will infect others. According to Dr. Robert Redfield, a specialist in infectious diseases at Walter Reed Army Medical Center, "The most important education message is to encourage widespread testing."

Testing could be expanded in a variety of ways. Voluntary testing could be even more strongly encouraged and facilitated. I believe it should be. And I think there is a good case to be made for proposals to make testing routine for hospital admissions; for persons receiving treatment at clinics, particularly those serving high-risk populations; for persons securing marriage licenses, and for those seeking admission to this country; and for all persons convicted of a crime upon imprisonment, and a second test prior to release.

All of these possibilities, and others, deserve to be explored. Is the failure of most states to offer even optional AIDS screening at venereal disease clinics sensible? I don't think so. In these states, anyone who comes to a clinic with a suspected venereal disease will be tested for a wide range of sexually transmitted diseases, but rarely for AIDS. That doesn't make sense. Many states require a blood test for syphilis to obtain a marriage license, but no test for AIDS is required. And where testing has taken place, only a handful of states offer to contact previous sexual partners of people known to be infected with the virus—what is known as contact notification. Shouldn't these individuals be told of their possible exposure to AIDS?

Why is there so much resistance to AIDS testing? Why is there so much resistance to at least limited disclosure of test results to, say, public health officials and sex partners? Opponents of routine testing offer several arguments against it. None is convincing.

One argument is that routine testing would drive the principal classes of AIDS victims (homosexuals and intravenous drug users) "underground," because they would be fearful of discrimination as a result of testing positive. First of all, even if some individuals did go underground, we would have to balance this fact with the crucial information more widespread routine testing would produce. This information would save lives. Second, the possibility that some individuals would avoid testing can be minimized by strong guarantees of confidentiality and nondiscrimination. Third, we would not, of course, eliminate voluntary AIDS testing sites even as we adopt a policy of routine testing. Routine testing would serve in conjunction with voluntary and even voluntary anonymous testing. And states and localities could, in certain circumstances, allow exceptions to routine testing. It is precisely by making testing *routine*, by dealing with it just as we treat other communicable diseases, that we will go a long way toward lessening the stigma that now surrounds AIDS tests.

Above all, I would point out that, by most estimates, the great majority of AIDS carriers—upwards of 90 percent—are currently unaware that they are infected. Routine testing at appropriate occasions—along with more widely available voluntary testing—would surely decrease the number of individuals who might be unwittingly spreading the disease.

A second argument made against routine testing is that the AIDS test is costly and unreliable. In fact, experience at the Department of Defense shows that testing can be done for less than $5 a person. The additional cost of counseling those who test positive is well worth the money. The AIDS tests are reliable and have been administered successfully. Moreover, a proper testing program includes provisions for double-checking positive test results.

A third argument against routine testing is that it could lead to violations of confidentiality, particularly as it relates to the notification of past sexual partners. A number of precautions can be taken to guard against this. For example, in many states today, if a person tests positive for syphilis, health authorities will ask for the names of people wth whom that person has been intimate. Then, without mentioning the name of the syphilis carrier, the health authorities will confidentially notify those people who may have contracted the disease and recommend that they be tested. This has long been standard public health practice. It can be done for AIDS as well. To protect others, it certainly should be done.

There are also strong arguments for considering superceding, in certain circumstances, the principle of confidentiality. After all, confidentiality, even in the medical profession, does not outweigh all other considerations. The American Medical Association's "Principles of Medical Ethics" recognizes that a physician may reveal otherwise confidential information if this is necessary to protect the welfare of another individual or the community. Several state court cases have recognized that such disclosures are not a breach of the physician's professional code if the disclosures are necessary to protect the public. Some of these cases have upheld disclosures by a physician concerning a patient's disease made to the patient's spouse. While these cases did not involve AIDS, their logic would seem to apply, at least in the absence of a state statute to the contrary.

In other significant cases it has been held that physicians have not only the authority, but a duty, to notify third parties (such as attendants, family members, and others in contact with a patient) of the risk of infection from a patient and that physicians may be held liable for breach of this duty. Indeed, according to Dr. Roy Schwarz, the American Medical Association's assistant executive vice-president for medical education and science, "When someone has the potential of transmitting the disease to someone who isn't infected, the second party has the right to know."

Now, these are not simply medical or legal issues. They are issues of public policy which require honest, open, and thoughtful debate. Such a debate would have to weigh competing principles and considerations, taking into account the claims of individual privacy versus the well-being of other individuals. I believe such a debate would lead us to reject, for example, the California law that makes it illegal to divulge results of an AIDS test to anyone without written permission. This law, as I understand it, means that unless the mother consents, a doctor delivering a baby cannot tell other medical personnel, including the child's pediatrician, if the mother has AIDS. It means a physician cannot inform past or present sex partners, unless the infected individual consents. Does this law sensibly balance the competing claims of the privacy of the patient and the well-being of others? I don't think so. The American College of Obstetricians and Gynecologists has recently called for expanded testing among high-risk women and has criticized some current state laws in which a doctor cannot, for example, inform a pediatrician or public health authorities about a new mother's AIDS test results.

Similarly, I doubt whether an open and honest debate would leave us in accord with a New York state policy that resulted in fifty prisoners who were afflicted with AIDS being released on parole without the state requiring disclosure of their condition to their spouses or lovers. As reported in the *New York Times*, one parole officer said, "I had one [parolee] assigned to me who simply didn't care. The guy was given about a year to live, and he was in total despair. He told me he was going to have sex with as many prostitutes as he could get his hands on, just to get even. What do I do, since he isn't violating his parole? He can kill someone, and we can't do anything about it." I doubt that this is the kind of public policy we want to condone.

Cases like these need to be addressed. We need to ask: Are we thinking through the costs, as well as the benefits, of these kinds of policies? Do we not need more testing? Is voluntary testing sufficient? How do we balance a desire to protect the confidentiality of AIDS carriers against our obligation to protect the health of other individuals? Can we not see to it that testing, contact notification, and the sharing of information can be conducted within strict safeguards to ensure that such measures are used solely as compelling public health considerations dictate? More generally, are we doing everything we can by way of public health and public policy measures to impede the spread of this terrible disease? Of course, there are limits to what we can do. But we must do what we can; and we cannot let the fact that many of these questions are difficult, and many of the choices hard, deter us from facing up to them.

I realize, of course, that I have touched on sensitive issues. So be it. We must not fear to raise these issues, to ask the hard questions, and to state in public the precise nature of the dilemmas and responsibilities that face us. The question of AIDS and the prevention of its spread cannot be treated as closed questions, as questions we are hesitant to address in this, an open society.

We have not had the open and honest debate on AIDS that the subject demands. The fear of seeming to be insensitive, intolerant, or mean-spirited has had an intimidating effect, a chilling effect, on public debate on AIDS. It is time that we tell the truth and face the facts about AIDS. The truth is this: AIDS kills. AIDS has changed the way we think about things. AIDS will profoundly affect the kinds of health and public policies we adopt. It is fruitless, indeed it is downright dangerous, to pretend we can conduct business as usual. As Secretary of Education, I must say that education can play a part; but I must also say that education cannot do it all. It is necessary to know the facts of the disease and how it is transmitted; such knowledge will help.* But a shift in behavior is required too, and education alone is not sufficient to that task. It is not true that knowledge of what is right always leads to proper action. Our job is to adjust our health and public policies to foster proper action, for the protection of all.

Physicians estimate—conservatively estimate—that by 1991 some 270,000 Americans will have been stricken with AIDS and some 180,000 will have died. That's more deaths than this country suffered in the Vietnam and Korean wars combined. And as Frank Polk, a leading AIDS researcher at Johns Hopkins University Medical School, has said, "The stakes are getting higher every day."

There are no easy answers, no medical miracles waiting on the horizon. There are only difficult decisions waiting to be made.

---

* In October 1987, the Education Department published a 28-page booklet about AIDS education, *AIDS and the Education of Our Children: A Guide for Parents and Teachers.* A free copy may be obtained by writing: Consumer Information Center, Dept. ED, Pueblo, CO 81009.

These are decisions that should not be left to politicians and advocacy groups alone. These decisions affect all of us, and they should be decided by all of us. We need to begin the hard work of forging a consensus on how to deal with AIDS. We need to develop policies that will contain the spread of this terrible disease, and that are consistent with both the public interest and our time-honored values.

So, let us get on with the task. The time is short, the threat is real, the consequences of our decisions are great. They involve nothing less than our lives, and the lives of our children.

HIGHER EDUCATION: PROMISE AND REALITY

THIRTEEN

Martin Luther King and the Liberal Arts *

IN HIS LANDMARK "Letter from Birmingham City Jail," Martin Luther King, Jr., distinguished between a just and an unjust law. Citing Thomas Aquinas, Reverend King explained that "a just law is a man-made code that squares with the moral law or the law of God. An unjust law is a mode that is out of harmony with the moral law. . . . Any law that uplifts human personality is just. Any law that degrades human personality is unjust." This distinction drawn by Reverend King has to do not only with laws but with the nature of government in general. For King was reminding us that democracy is more than a complex set of checks and balances designed to reconcile majority rule and minority rights. Democracy is also a form of government that seeks to uplift the human personality; a form of government that encourages everyone—rich and poor, black and white, male and female—to develop his or her potential to the utmost. Indeed, broadly conceived, democracy is not simply a form of government; it is a way of life, and—if you will allow me a new phrase—a way of ideas.

Spelman College is an institution that embodies many of the most important principles championed by Martin Luther King. Founded in the basement of Atlanta's Friendship Baptist Church

* This chapter is based on an address delivered at Spelman College, Atlanta, Georgia, January 13, 1986.

in 1881, Spelman has dedicated itself to the great task of uplifting the human personality. Its cardinal assumption has always been that the daughters, granddaughters, and great-granddaughters of slaves are no less entitled than the children of the privileged to be exposed to the very best that has been thought, written, and expressed about the human experience. This equality of concern makes Spelman a very special place—exactly the kind of place with which one would expect the King family to be closely associated.

And, in fact, the family of Martin Luther King *has* been closely associated with Spelman. King's mother, Alberta Williams King, graduated from Spelman High School. His sister, Christine King Farris, is associate professor of education at Spelman and director of the reading program. His daughter, Bernice Albertine King, recently graduated from Spelman; his niece, Angela Christine Farris is currently a senior at Spelman. And King himself delivered the Founders Day address at Spelman in 1960.

In recent years, however, the philosophy which informs Spelman College has occasionally come under attack. What is so important, critics have asked, about exposing young black women to the great books of the past? With so many urgent tasks facing the black community, so many problems that cry out to be resolved, shouldn't students pursue a more "practical," more career-oriented course of study? Isn't all this attention to history, philosophy, and literature—to the humanities and the liberal arts—more of a luxury than a necessity, something which American blacks, at this point in their history, can ill afford?

I'd like to address these criticisms. Moreover, I'd like to address them not in an abstract, theoretical way, but by reference to the life and work of Reverend King—a life and work infused to a remarkable degree by our highest intellectual traditions. Indeed, it may seem ironic to some that one of the few men who can claim to have had a profound effect on the practices of this free society did so by training himself, immersing himself, in what some might call "dead books."

Martin Luther King was born in Atlanta, Georgia, on January 15, 1929, a time when southern blacks lived under a state of racial siege known as Jim Crow. Much has been said about Jim Crow, and I will confine myself here to one statistic: between 1882 and 1946, 4,715 people, about three-quarters of them black, were lynched in the United States. Some of these lynchings were carried out by small groups of vigilantes, others were the work of frenzied mobs. Either way, these crimes often enjoyed the toleration or even the approval of local authorities. That was Jim Crow.

Though much of public opinion was outraged by these crimes, little was done about them. Thus, Jim Crow became an entrenched way of life throughout the South, a system based on segregated housing, segregated schools, segregated restaurants, segregated theaters, segregated restrooms, segregated drinking fountains—segregated everything. Yet not all southern blacks would accommodate themselves to this way of life, and among those very brave men and women who would not do so was Martin Luther King, Sr. In his book *Stride Toward Freedom,* King recalls this story about his father:

> I remembered a trip to a downtown shoestore with father when I was still small. We had sat down in the first empty seats at the front of the store. A young white clerk came up and murmured politely: "I'll be happy to wait on you if you'll just move to those seats in the rear." My father answered, "There's nothing wrong with these seats. We're quite comfortable here." "Sorry," said the clerk, "but you'll have to move." "We'll either buy shoes sitting here," my father retorted, "or we won't buy shoes at all." Whereupon he took me by the hand and walked out of the store. This was the first time I had ever seen my father so angry. I still remember walking down the street beside him as he muttered, "I don't care how long I have to live with this system, I will never accept it."

With such a father, it is no wonder that young Martin Luther King grew up determined never to accept Jim Crow. On the contrary, he desperately wanted to help change the way blacks were being treated. But how? There were so many contending philosophies within the black community, so many different points of view. Should he embrace Booker T. Washington's gradualism? Marcus Garvey's "Back to Africa" movement? A. Philip Randolph's direct action campaigns? The NAACP's legal strategy? Or should he, the son of a relatively well-to-do family, take up the concept advocated by W. E. B. Du Bois, that black progress could only come with the development of an educated black elite, the so-called Talented Tenth? There seemed to be no firm ground on which to map a strategy, no compass to steer by.

Martin Luther King graduated from Morehouse College in June 1948, with a Bachelor of Arts degree in sociology. Initially, studying sociology had seemed to him a way of sorting through the dilemmas he was wrestling with, but he soon grew disillusioned with it. He particularly objected to sociology's tendency to reduce people to mere numbers, and he complained about the "apathetic fallacy of statistics." Moreover, while at Morehouse he came under the influence of a remarkable educator, Dr. Benjamin E. Mays, who inspired him to change his area of study. And so, when he entered Crozer Theological Seminary the following September, he began to immerse himself in the writings of the great political philosophers, "from Plato and Aristotle," as he wrote later, "down to Rousseau, Hobbes, Bentham, Mill and Locke." Here, with these teachers, was planted the seed not of a contemplative life but of a life of action—a life of thoughtful devotion to political reform, to the pursuit of justice.

What do the writings of Plato and Aristotle, Greek philosophers who lived and taught more than two thousand years ago, have to do with the plight of a young black American growing up under Jim Crow in the middle of the twentieth century? Why did Martin Luther King immerse himself in what some call "esoteric" and "irrelevant" writings when there were so many urgent problems which he himself was determined to confront? Was his study of philosophy a form of escapism, a means of evading the problems of real life?

Of course not. On the contrary, Martin Luther King turned to the great philosophers because he needed to know the answers to certain questions. What is justice? What should be loved? What deserves to be defended? What can I know? What should I do? What may I hope for? What is man? These questions are not simply intellectual diversions, but have engaged thoughtful human beings in all places and in all ages. As a result of the ways in which these questions have been answered, civilizations have emerged, nations have developed, wars have been fought, and people have lived contentedly or miserably. And as a result of the way in which Martin Luther King eventually answered these questions, Jim Crow was destroyed and American history was transformed.

Three figures in American history fascinate me—James Madison, Abraham Lincoln, and Martin Luther King. I have studied their lives fairly closely. Each profoundly affected a different century in our nation's life. Each exercised political leadership. Each exercised moral leadership. Each exercised intellectual leadership. And each of these men demonstrated that it is ideas which ultimately move society—ideas contained in the great works of Western civilization, ideas encountered through education.

A great Italian philosopher and historian, Benedetto Croce, once observed, all history has the character of contemporary history. By this he meant that since history deals with the actions of human beings, and since human beings haven't changed much over the years, all of history illuminates our current dilemmas and perplexities. For much the same reason, I think it can be said that all of philosophy is contemporary philosophy, all of literature is contemporary literature, and all of art is contemporary art. Indeed, all the great writers, thinkers, and artists of the past are our contemporaries, in the sense that they all have much to teach us, if only we allow them to.

And so the young Martin Luther King went with his problems and perplexities and the palpable passions of his time to the great teachers of mankind—and they did not disappoint him. Just as, two hundred years before him, the young James Madison had gone with *his* problems to the great teachers of mankind. Just as, one hundred years before him, the young Abraham Lincoln had gone with *his* problems to the great teachers of mankind. And just as James Madison (with Thomas Jefferson) became the greatest exponent of the American dream in the eighteenth century, just as Abraham Lincoln became the greatest exponent of the American dream in the nineteenth century, so Martin Luther King became its greatest advocate and articulator in our time.

How did Martin Luther King come to understand the American dream? Let me quote a passage from a commencement address delivered by Dr. King at Lincoln University on June 6, 1961:

> One of the first things we notice in this dream is an amazing universalism. [The Declaration of Independence] does not say some men [are created equal], but it says all men. It does not say all white men, but it says all men, which includes black men. It does not say all Gentiles, but it says all men, which in-

cludes Jews. It does not say all Protestants, but it says all men, which includes Catholics.

And there is another thing we see in this dream that ultimately distinguishes democracy and our form of government from all of the totalitarian regimes that emerge in history. It says that each individual has certain basic rights that are neither conferred by nor derived from the state. To discover where they came from it is necessary to move back behind the dim mist of eternity, for they are God-given. Very seldom if ever in the history of the world has a sociopolitical document expressed in such profoundly eloquent and unequivocal language the dignity and the worth of the human personality. The American dream reminds us that every man is heir to the legacy of worthiness.

These words speak from the past to the present; and they do so most eloquently. Martin Luther King's education imbued his words with historical perspective and intellectual power.

"Every man is heir to the legacy of worthiness." To southern blacks who had been oppressed for decades—indeed, for centuries—King's message, expressed, like the Declaration of Independence, in "profoundly eloquent and unequivocal language," brought a renewed sense of dignity and self-worth. Thanks to what a close aide to Dr. King, Bayard Rustin, has called a "tremendous facility for giving people the feeling that they could be bigger and stronger and more courageous than they thought they could be," Martin Luther King and his Southern Christian Leadership Conference succeeded in creating a disciplined mass movement of southern blacks to protest Jim Crow. And as Rustin has further noted, the black people mobilized by the SCLC were not hard-core political activists but "ordinary people—church women, workers, and students. There had been nothing in the annals of American social struggle to equal this phenomenon." And, let me add, there may never be again.

But Rev. King did more than mobilize black people to confront the injustice of Jim Crow. By his personal example, by the power of his words and his actions, he succeeded in mobilizing the majority of white Americans behind a national consensus to destroy Jim Crow. And once this *national* consensus of blacks and whites had been forged, Jim Crow was doomed, its authority, in a phrase St. Augustine borrowed from Cicero, no more than that of a "den of robbers," sustained by physical intimidation alone.

Having very briefly reviewed some of King's great accomplishments, let me return to the question with which I began. In light of the grave and urgent problems confronting the black community, why should black women acquire a liberal arts education? Why should they not pursue a more "practical" course of study?

The answer to this question emerges very clearly from a study of Martin Luther King's life. For what such a study reveals is a young man deeply committed to helping his people, but unsure of how to do so. It shows us a young man thoroughly familiar with the writings of black leaders and intellectuals, yet uncertain whether any of these leaders and intellectuals had hit upon the "solution" to Jim Crow. It shows us a courageous, intellectually independent young man, someone who had to work things out for himself. And finally, it shows us a blessed young man, blessed in his parents, blessed in his choice of college, blessed in his teachers, and blessed in finding older mentors to help ease his way. Here was an extraordinary combination of talent, will, mind, heart, and grace. That such a young man ultimately found his way to the great thinkers and teachers of humanity seems, in retrospect, almost inevitable. For what is philosophy, what are the liberal arts in general, if not the means by which civilized human beings talk to each other about the things that matter most? And what are the things that matter most, if not the things that preoccupied Martin Luther King: justice, human rights, freedom, and the brotherhood of man under God?

King turned to the liberal arts because he was in search not only of knowledge, but of wisdom. He understood that the purpose of an education is not merely to prepare us for a job, but to prepare us for life—for the eminently practical tasks of living well, thinking wisely, and acting sensibly. It is in approaching these tasks that the humanities become an invaluable companion. King's mentor, Benjamin Mays, put it very well. At Morehouse, Dr. Mays used to say, he was not turning out doctors or lawyers or preachers; he was turning out men.

Having worked closely in the past with Spelman's president, Donald Stewart, I know that he shares these sentiments, that he too is committed to helping turn out morally alert, intellectually mature young women capable of playing a vital role in the life of our democracy. And I know, too, that Dr. Stewart shares my view that the humanities speak to us regardless of race, sex, or creed. They speak to our condition as human beings; they speak to us in terms that we share, if not as a species, then certainly as a nation.

We are, as Walt Whitman observed, "a nation of nations." Diversity is a fundamental element of our culture, and one that we rightly celebrate. But we must remember that the "E Pluribus Unum" that defines us as a nation denotes unity as well as plurality. There is a time for noting what makes us different, and a time for recognizing what we share.

It was to the common code of American culture—the ideals of the Declaration of Independence, with their roots in the Judeo-Christian tradition—that Martin Luther King appealed when he declared, "I have a dream." Common culture—common values, common knowledge, a common language—is essential to sharing dreams and to discussing differences. There are some things that we must all learn and learn together. The humanities can help us in this.

Of course, most of us cannot hope to accomplish even a fraction of what Martin Luther King achieved. But all of us do have an obligation, to ourselves if to no one else, to acquaint ourselves with our civilization's highest ideals and aspirations.

King lived less than forty years—not a very long time. On April 3, 1968—the day before he was shot—he spoke at a meeting in Memphis, Tennessee. This is what he said:

> I don't know what will happen now. We've got some difficult days ahead. But it doesn't matter with me now. Because I've been to the mountaintop. And I don't mind. Like anybody, I would like to live a long life. Longevity has its place. But I'm not concerned about that now. I just want to do God's will. And he's allowed me to go up to the mountain. And I've looked over. And I've seen the promised land. I may not get there with you. But I want you to know tonight, that we, as a people will get to the promised land.

No, we haven't reached the promised land yet, but thanks to Reverend King, thanks to great institutions of learning like Spelman and Morehouse, we can all see it now. And with God's help, the day is coming when we Americans, as a people, will surely get there.

The Lorraine Motel, a modest building in Memphis, is the place where Martin Luther King was shot. A commemorative plaque bears a simple inscription from the Book of Genesis: "And they said one to another, Behold, this dreamer cometh. Come now therefore, and let us slay him . . . and we shall see what will become of his dreams." Note the tentative nature of the final clause—"and we shall see what will become of his dreams." What will become of his dreams is up to the rest of us. It is not yet determined. But our own dreams will be determined in no small part by how we choose to educate our children. For education is about skills and standards and know-how and jobs—yes, all of these—but it is also about dreams and about dreamers. I close with a line of Wordsworth: "What we have loved, others will love, and we will teach them how." And I say, what Martin Luther King did dream, others may dream, but we must teach them how.

FOURTEEN

A Matter of Quality*

I ONCE FOUND MYSELF talking with a high-ranking education official of a nation very different from our own, a powerful nation, but one which has never acknowledged the political principles we in this country hold to be self-evident. He had understood me to be a critic of American higher education, so he asked me what I took to be the system's worst faults.

Excuse me, I told him, but you misunderstand. What you overheard were the words of a man speaking candidly to those whom he proudly considers his own. "Proudly" because he knows that the flaws he sees at close quarters are significant flaws, but that they are nevertheless flaws in a very great structure, an unsurpassed wonder of the world. No system of higher education, I said, has ever afforded greater intellectual freedom to students or their teachers. No system can boast nearly as much public and private support, or half the variety and color. For all its deficiencies, ours is the world's greatest system of higher education.

This system, I continued, is remarkable. Our colleges, community colleges, and universities enroll 12 million students; three out of five of our high school graduates enter institutions of higher learning, a greater proportion than in any other industrialized

* This chapter is based on an address delivered to the American Council on Education, Miami Beach, Florida, October 28, 1985.

nation. They choose from among more than 3,000 colleges and universities whose total budget exceeds $85.5 billion, and which employ more than 700,000 professors. This massive system of higher education is an indispensable foundation of our economic progress and national well-being.

Furthermore, at its best this system is better than anyone else's. We have the best research and the most superb teaching. We offer more second chances, more choices, more ability to tailor one's educational experiences to one's changing goals and circumstances throughout life. In short, our system of higher education has given more to our people than has any other in all of history.

These are truths so obvious that we seldom feel the need to restate them. Only when we speak to an outsider are we reminded of how extraordinary a system we have. But within the family we tend to use a different voice. And this is appropriate. Here constructive criticism is needed to guard against the danger of complacency. I have been critical of some aspects of American higher education since long before becoming Secretary of Education. But when I speak as a critic—as, I trust, a constructive critic—I speak as a member of the family. I am a product of the academy. I found intellectual nourishment there. I taught there. I administered there. I am, to use a phrase I have used in a different context, "blood of the blood, flesh of the flesh." And so I feel entitled to speak freely, even critically, to my colleagues.

The recent reports on higher education have been, to all intents and purposes, products of the academy. They have been addressed by its members to its members. But now we are beginning to hear other voices as well. The National Governors' Association has named upgrading higher education one of its major initiatives in the coming years. It has resolved to investigate what states can do to improve consumer information about higher education, assessment of undergraduate performance, and institutional management. Governor Thomas Kean of New Jersey has said that the Education Commission of the States should "think deeply about how to inspire effective state action to improve undergraduate education."

This recent surge of gubernatorial interest is significant. It is no coincidence that we are hearing these new voices outside the walls of the academy, voices of people who are concerned about higher education and are seeking to involve themselves in reform efforts. Is it, in fact, a sequence that parallels the one followed by the recent reform of secondary education.

I believe that it will be of no more use here than it was with secondary education to linger over the question of whether conditions are worse than they once were. The relevant fact is that they could be better. It is generally agreed, for example, that many of our graduates do not seem to possess the knowledge, skills, and, in some cases, the character and civic virtues that should constitute a highly educated person. The evidence is often fragmentary and impressionistic. We have all heard stories of the college senior who cannot place France on a map or World War I in the right century. Some of the evidence is more tangible; student performance on eleven out of fifteen major subject area tests of the Graduate Record Examination declined between 1964 and 1982.

As college costs continue to rise, parents are beginning to ask whether they are getting their money's worth. They are saying college is too expensive. Witness, for example, the book by the *New York Times* education writer Edward Fiske, *The Best Buys in College Education.* As one college president has said, "The book exemplifies the changing mood among parents that price is becoming important. Twenty years ago it was not a great issue." I agree. And the more price becomes an issue, the more the quality of the product becomes an issue.

Quality of the product—quality of the education received—this is the issue. In recent years we have concentrated on the *quantity* of higher education; we speak proudly of the number of our universities, the number of their programs, the number of students to whom they are accessible. The Census Bureau has recently told us that, in terms of the number of Americans receiving high school and college diplomas, we are the most educated people in the world. Let's make sure we are also the *best* educated in the world.

We must always remember that access is important. But this must mean access to quality. Recently, the Southern Regional Educational Board observed that "the quality and meaning of undergraduate education has fallen to a point at which mere access has lost much of its value." As we strive to maintain access, we must make sure that we are working for access to a worthwhile educational experience.

Traditionally, the quality of colleges and universities has been measured by available resources—the number of faculty members with Ph.D.s, the faculty–student ratio, dollars spent per student, size of the endowment, freshman SAT scores, number of volumes on the library shelves. But the shortcomings noted by the various critics do not trace back to the quantity of resources or other institutional "inputs." Virtually nobody, at least nobody outside the academy, believes that, in general, resources are lacking. American parents and taxpayers have been willing to spend the thousands of dollars that it costs to educate a college student. American corporations have been generous; the $1.25 billion they gave to colleges last year was 14 percent more than they gave the year before. Corporate support has more than doubled since the 1978–79 academic year. Foundations gave over $1 billion last year, up 6.2 percent from the year before. Yes, in some places more resources are needed. Yes, in some places more are deserved. But the case cannot be made that the American people have been ungenerous to higher education. They haven't, and we all know that.

The current shortcomings of higher education must be addressed by focusing not on inputs, but on the quality of processes within the institution. The various national reports, for example, have blamed most problems on indecision, lackluster teaching, lack of curricular coherence, and lack of clear and steadfast standards. But we must understand that, from the perspective of society at large, the important inadequacies are not so much in the processes as in outcome and performance. At the undergraduate level, we might, at the risk of oversimplifying, state the fundamental problem as this: we are uncertain what we think our students should learn, how best to teach it to them, and how to be sure when they have learned it.

Stated this way, the criticisms don't sound so different from the dominant criticisms of secondary education. Consider, for example, this finding from *A Nation At Risk:*

> Secondary school curricula have been homogenized, diluted, and diffused to the point that they no longer have a central purpose. In effect, we have a cafeteria-style curriculum in

which the appetizers and desserts can easily be mistaken for
the main courses.

And now this statement from the Association of American Colleges report, *Integrity in the College Curriculum:*

> As for what passes for a college curriculum, almost anything
> goes. We have reached a point at which we are more confident
> about the length of a college education than its content and
> purpose . . . [T]he major in most colleges is little more than
> a gathering of courses taken in one department, lacking depth
> and structure. . . . The absence of a rationale for the major
> becomes transparent in college catalogues where the essential
> message embedded in all the fancy prose is: pick eight of the
> following. And "the following" might literally be over a hun-
> dred courses, all served up as equals.

Of course, a college and a high school have as many differences as similarities. Among those differences is that in college we
are dealing for the most part with adults who may have definite
opinions about what they should be learning. We rightly prize the
diversity and flexibility of higher education, permitting choices
and not forcing everyone into the same mold. Furthermore, since
students are not obliged to attend college at all, institutions of
higher education must contend with a buyers' market in which
they may have few customers if they aren't reasonably responsive
to demand.

Even given these differences, however, higher education can
learn a lesson from the reform movement taking place at the elementary and secondary level. In what is now called "effective
schools research," reformers have been successful in studying
schools that appear to produce good students and then identifying
the common characteristics of those institutions. And, as it turns
out, among the characteristics of effective schools is a willingness to
define educational goals, to assess performance in meeting those
goals, and to make the results available to the community.

Can higher education do the same? Yes, I believe that a number of criticisms can be met and higher education can be strengthened if our institutions do a more conscientious job of stating their
goals, of gauging their success in relation to those goals, and of

making the results available to everyone. In short, what is needed is a method of assessing student learning and development that sheds light on the performance of particular institutions. As the report by the Association of American Colleges stated: "As difficult as it may be to develop the most searching and appropriate methods of evaluation and assessment, an institution that lacks refined instruments of program evaluation and rigorous instruments of student assessment is contributing to the debasement of baccalaureate education."

Perhaps the worst of all possible worlds for the prospective undergraduate is a landscape barren of real information with which to make informed choices, but instead littered with trendy indicators of campus popularity and status. No one wants high school seniors depending on slick publications that claim to "tell it like it really is." Here I refer not to Mr. Fiske's book, but ones like a recent popular guide that informs students which campus has the best salad bar and where the most promiscuous students are.

It is only fair, given the cost of a college education, that there exist some sort of consumer protection. Above all, it is needed for the sake of students from less financially fortunate homes, students for whom a college education may be the best hope for success. They should not be left to whim or hearsay or false assertions like "expensive is necessarily better," only to discover later that they aren't getting what they bargained for. Indeed, any family that makes sacrifices for its children's education—and today most do—deserves to have reliable information with which to make choices.

The Department of Education has an obligation to the students it assists with financial aid, and to the taxpayers whose funds it disburses, to suggest better means by which the higher education consumer can be confident he or she is purchasing a sound product. There are several ways in which we are already involved in the assessment of higher education. We gather data, and we conduct and support research and development.

We are willing to do more. We are prepared to join in cooperative ventures with the higher education community as a whole, with major segments, even with individual institutions. We are peculiarly suited to making broad assessments of our colleges' success in imparting particular skills and knowledge; we could, for example, extend the National Assessment on Educational Progress beyond age seventeen to post-college years. But we in the federal government will not play a primary role in the assessment of colleges and universities. It would not be appropriate; it would not be desirable; above all, it would not be as effective as initiatives undertaken by our colleges and universities themselves.

Apart from the basic skills and knowledge that we expect all universities to impart, there are individual institutional goals that vary enormously from school to school. It is only sensible that each school assess its own progress toward those goals. This is the surest way to turn the lofty statements of college catalogs into actual classroom practice. If we are to keep our promises, we must be willing to shed light on our shortcomings, and on our efforts to turn shortcomings into strengths. Such candor will not harm anyone's admission pool.

Such acknowledgment is the surest way to maintain institutional integrity; it is also the best way to maintain institutional sovereignty. For if institutions do not assess their own performance, others—either state or commercial outfits—will most likely do it for them.

Here is one more lesson to be learned from elementary and secondary education. The failure of school leadership to specify goals in ways that would allow judgments on performance has led, in many cases, to decisions being taken out of their hands. The same fate could befall higher education if its leaders do not accept the necessity of basic standards, and criteria.

Assessments might use a variety of methods—standardized tests, interviews or questionnaires, reviews of students' written work over four years, reviews of extracurricular activity, studies of alumni and dropouts, surveys of students' use of time, surveys of graduates' use of time. Some results could be expressed in numerical terms; many obviously could not. In large, complex universities, assessment might be conducted separately by schools, colleges, or departments. But no matter what the form, judgments must be made so that institutions can assure the public that they are doing what they say they are doing.

I have compared the challenge before American higher education to that currently being met by our secondary schools. I would like to note one final point of correspondence. In recent years, we have learned that one of the qualities most essential to a good high school is a good principal. Likewise, at the college level the involvement of deans, provosts, and presidents will prove fundamental to producing effective schools. This nation has grown accustomed to looking to its colleges and universities for direction on a host of important issues; I am confident that here too the leadership of the higher education community will not be found lacking.

It is no accident that the world's greatest system of higher education is the prize of the world's greatest democracy. That system owes its life to a spirit of public generosity and enthusiasm for the pursuit of knowledge. Americans owe much to higher education, but higher education owes Americans even more. Such debts are repaid only by offering the best one can muster.

FIFTEEN

The Rhetoric and Reality
of Higher Education*

DURING THE Roman Saturnalia even slaves could speak freely. On the occasion of Harvard College's 350th anniversary, let me invoke ancient custom and ask that, I, a public servant, be permitted to speak freely. And so I shall speak about the condition, as I see it, of American higher education today. I am not confident that this condition is an entirely healthy one.

I want to discuss the question of the extent to which our colleges and universities contribute to the fulfillment, to the betterment, of the lives of their students, of the young men and women given over to their charge. I have been concerned with this question since I was an undergraduate and then a graduate student; but perhaps not so intensely until I arrived at Harvard in 1968. I came as a law student, and became also a proctor in Matthews Hall, and a tutor in social studies. I had a good time, and learned some things and treasure some memories.

Let me mention one set of memories in particular. My job as a freshman proctor was far and away the best part of my years at Harvard. I made some fast friends, I learned a great deal, and I think I was able to be of some actual help to those whose well-

* This chapter is based on an address delivered at Harvard University, Cambridge, Massachusetts, October 10, 1986.

being was my direct and ongoing responsibility. Every year, from the photographs and records that were available, I memorized my freshmen before they arrived, so that I could greet them by name and be somewhat familiar with their interests and talents. I made it a point not to conform to the pretentious practice of keeping proctor's office hours—mere graduate or law students acting like full professors; my freshmen were always welcome in my room, and they made use of this welcome. We spent a lot of time together, at parties, at our own softball and football games, and in serious and not-so-serious discussion. To some of them, I'm proud to say, I occasionally gave a hard time. I was tough on drugs, and I would not sign course-change cards if I thought a student was going after gut courses or otherwise undercutting his academic opportunities.

Proctoring was the highlight of my experience at Harvard, though I enjoyed the tutoring as well, and law school was at least interesting. But out of these various Harvard experiences, and especially from the illuminating vantage point of a proctor, I formed some notions both about this university and about American higher education in general. My subsequent experiences at other colleges and universities have served to strengthen these notions into convictions.

One of my fundamental convictions is this: there is an extraordinary gap between the rhetoric and the reality of American higher education. The gap is so wide, in fact, that we face the real possibility—not today, perhaps not tomorrow, but someday—of an erosion of public support for the enterprise.

The rhetoric of contemporary higher education, the terms in which its practitioners and advocates speak of it, is often exceedingly pious, self-congratulatory, and suffused with an aura of moral superiority. The spokesmen for higher education tend to invoke the mission of the university as if they were reciting the Nicene Creed: one, holy, universal, and apostolic church. To be sure, being modern and sophisticated, they also know the rhetorical uses of a little well-placed deprecation, and they can speak winningly of the need for constant self-inspection and self-improvement. But try, as I have tried, to criticize American higher education by the one yardstick that matters—namely, the relative success or failure of our colleges and universities at discharging the educational responsibilities that they bear—and from the reaction, you would think I had hurled a rock through the stained-glass window of a cathedral. The response to my criticism was not "Prove it" or "You're wrong for the following reasons"; it was more like "How dare you"—or "Who do you think you are?" Well, I know who I am, having been a student at three colleges and universities, and a teacher at six. I know who I am, but does the university know what *it* is? The university claims to educate, to improve the minds—even the hearts—of young men and women. Sometimes it does this, certainly—but not as often, or as wholeheartedly, or as purposefully and successfully as it should.

Let's take Harvard as an example. Considering the vast sums that parents pay for the privilege of sending their children to a college like Harvard, it may seem gauche or impertinent to ask whether the sacrifice is matched by the value of the education received in exchange. But the question is nevertheless worth asking, for the fact is that neither those fees themselves, nor a $3.1 billion endowment, nor a library system staggering in its holdings, nor research laboratories and scientific facilities that are the envy of the world, nor renowned centers for the study of domestic and international affairs, nor first-class museums and theaters, nor a faculty justly acclaimed for its scholarship and intellectual brilliance, nor even, for that matter, a brainy and resourceful student body—the fact is that none of these things is evidence that Harvard or any similarly situated university is really fulfilling its obligation to its students of seeing to it that when they leave after four years, they leave as educated men and women.

That Harvard is a place where one *can* get a good education, no one can doubt. With the presence on one campus of all those resources I've just enumerated, and especially the final two items on the list—the bright young men and women whom the college attracts as students, and the gifted scholars with whom they are placed in proximity—exciting things will occur. It's a good bet. But it does not occur in all cases—and I would fault Harvard and other universities for this: there's not much effort to see to it, systematically and devotedly, that real education occurs. Under the justification of deferring to individual decisions and choices, much is left to chance. Sometimes a proctor, a professor, a dean steps in and takes a real interest in a student's education—but that's often the luck of the draw.

Our students deserve better. They deserve a university's sustained attention to their intellectual and moral well-being. And they deserve a good general education—at a minimum, a systematic familiarization with our Western tradition of learning: with the classical and Jewish-Christian heritage, the facts of American and European history, the political organization of Western societies, the great works of Western art and literature, the major achievements of the scientific disciplines. In short, the basic body of knowledge which universities once took it upon themselves as their obligation to transmit, in the name of a liberal education, from ages past to ages present and future.

As the distinguished historian James H. Billington has remarked, American universities have as a rule given up on this once central task—with the result that not only do students now tend to lack a knowledge of their own tradition, they often have no standpoint from which to appreciate any other tradition, or even to *have* a sense of tradition. Billington characterizes the typical undergraduate curriculum of today as a "smorgasbord." If this Scandinavian metaphor betrays too Western a bias, I would propose instead the metaphor of an old-style Chinese menu, the kind where a customer could pick this from column A and that from column B. Whatever may be said of this as a meal, it is not a model for a college curriculum.

But, one might respond, Harvard has a core curriculum. Well, I could respond in turn, does it? There is a symbolic nod, a feint, in the direction of a core curriculum. I have studied the Harvard catalog, and I agree that under the heading "core curriculum" we find an agglomeration of courses, many of them obviously meaty and important, taught by eminent scholars, on a wide variety of subjects. But, it seems to me, they could more appropriately find their place among the individual offerings of the various departments of instruction, from where, indeed, they give every appearance of having been plucked, only to be regrouped in new combinations. In what sense do these courses constitute a *core*—i.e., the central, foundational part of a liberal education? Some of the courses are truly core courses—and my sense is that in fact students,

to their credit, often flock to such classes. But they do not constitute a true core curriculum—i.e., a set of fundamental courses, ordered, purposive, coherent. I cannot discern such a core curriculum here.

Now despite this, many Harvard students get an education—or
at least they learn a lot. And, of course, there is a limit to what any
curriculum can accomplish. But if Harvard were more intentional
about it, more committed to ensuring that its undergraduates receive an education commensurate with the promise held out by
the core curriculum, it would be doing even better by its students,
and it would set a clearer example for all the institutions that look
to it. There are too many intellectual and educational casualties
among the student body of Harvard. Of course there would be
some under any plan; but there are more than there have to be,
and that's because luck, serendipity, chance, peer pressure, and a
kind of institutional negligence—often a very high-minded negligence—are not the best guarantors of a general education. Some
people don't get educated here—too many for the greatest university in the country. If when we take their money we say to parents
and taxpayers and donors that we'll educate their sons and daughters, let's do so. Let's do what we promise.

After all, American colleges and universities are quick to pro-
claim their duty to address all sorts of things that are wrong in the
world, to speak truth to those in power, to discourse on the complex social and moral issues beyond their walls, and to instruct
political and business and religious leaders on the proper path to
follow. But they have a prior duty, which is to see to the education of the young people in their charge—this is, after all, what
they are paid for. Some do—perhaps especially the smaller, less
famous institutions. But too often our institutions, especially our
most prestigious universities, fail in the discharge of their educational responsibilities. And they ought to be held to account for
this—not just by parents and trustees and donors and taxpayers,
but above all by students.

I was interested to read in the *Chronicle of Higher Education* of a recent comprehensive survey of undergraduates that
found the following: two-fifths reported that *no* professor at their
institution took a "special personal interest" in their academic progress; fewer than one-fifth rated their institution's academic advi-

sory programs "highly adequate," while nearly three-fifths rated them merely "adequate" or worse. Students should not accept this state of affairs as inevitable or preordained. I think that demanding greater guidance, a more serious assumption of responsibility by their institutions, is a worthy cause for student activism. Commencement exercises at Harvard College used to conclude—perhaps they still do—with the president welcoming the new graduates into the company of educated men and women. If students feel that their years at Harvard are failing to prepare them adequately for membership in that privileged company, they should let Harvard know.

Let me add that Harvard would, I think, be prepared to listen. One approach that may help foster quality and focus and purpose in undergraduate education goes by the name of assessment—that is, assessing what students actually learn. I suggested, near the beginning of my tenure as Secretary of Education, that more attention to this issue might be desirable. At the time, many in higher education refused even to consider it. But I do want to pay tribute to Harvard's president, my former crackerjack labor-law teacher, Derek Bok. He thinks the question of assessing quality is important, as he said in his most recent annual report, and he's beginning to do something about it, sponsoring a faculty seminar, among other things, at Harvard. Good for him. That's leadership. I hope others will follow—and we in the Department of Education stand ready to help.

Students should make other demands of colleges and universities as well. William James said the purpose of a college education is to help you to know a good man when you see him. (We can add "and a good woman.") He said a college education's best claim is that it helps one to value what deserves to be valued: "The only rational ground for pre-eminent admiration of any single college," James said, speaking of Harvard, "would be its pre-eminent spiritual tone." And James warned that all too often, "to be a college man, even a Harvard man, affords no sure guarantee for anything but a more educated cleverness in the service of popular idols and vulgar ends."

Notice that James is talking about both intellectual *and* moral discernment. What of moral discernment in particular? Most of our colleges would not dream of claiming to offer a moral education to their students, to their charges. Most do not seek to improve the individual moral sense of their students, much less their faculty. But there is no shortage of moralizing and moral posturing—especially the kind that does not cost anything of the individual, that does not take time or self-denial or effort. Chekhov said you can't become a saint through the sins of others, but many seem to think that's just how you do it. I remember some teachers in the seventies who were at a fever pitch over international injustices and the welfare of others in general, but in particular they did not want to give much time to those on their own campus whom they were charged to help. The advantage of a concern for justice in general, for justice somewhere else, is that it takes less time than pursuing justice in particular, and it has the added benefit of not interfering with meals, socializing, and other engagements.

Now, where do our colleges and universities stand on the issues of their responsibility to protect their students and their obligation to foster moral discernment in their students? With the exception of a few places—mostly religious or military institutions, I gather—higher education is silent. Many colleges freely dispense guidance to those beyond their walls, and such guidance is to be welcomed in a free society; but colleges that aim, as they might put it, to "lead" society's conscience on various social problems should not, when faced by a real problem within their walls, duck or throw up their hands. When it comes to drugs on campus, too many college presidents say, well, that's a society-wide problem, there's little we can do about it. This unaccustomed modesty is puzzling. I think moral responsibility begins at home. To be interested in broader issues is fine, but to neglect one's basic responsibilities is not. It is true that dealing with the drug problem requires a more sustained effort than signing a petition or mounting a demonstration; it requires individual and institutional time and long-term commitment. These have not been forthcoming on many of our campuses.

Earlier I compared the modern university with the old church. Although I am known as a friend of religion, let me say this: the self-righteousness that has given so many religious institutions a bad name has found an even more secure and hospitable home in the modern university. But in the old church most divines did not forget that the first injunction was, Heal thyself; they knew they had to attend to their own souls before they preached to the outside world. The residents of the modern university all too often take it upon themselves to preach, without even a cursory acknowledgment that they should first attend to healing themselves.

There is another analogy that can be drawn between the contemporary university and the old church. The church fell into some disrepute because its exhortations to poverty and holiness were too often belied by the worldliness and sumptuousness of its clerics. Similarly, American higher education simply refuses to acknowledge the obvious fact that, in general, it is rich. Whether this refusal is due to calculation or self-deception, I do not know, but in all the debates over student aid and federal tax policy, somehow this basic fact has been buried. Now, reasonable people can differ over student aid or tax policies—but these differences should be based on facts. And the fact is that the American people have been very generous to higher education.

From all the publicity, you would think that hosts of institutions are on the brink of collapse, others near the abyss; but this is not so. The number of institutions of higher education in the United States has increased from 1,852 in 1950 to 2,230 in 1965 to 3,231 in 1980 to 3,331 today. The number of public institutions continues to increase; the number of private institutions continues to increase. So let's not pretend this is a shrinking enterprise, in a perilous state.

And let's not pretend the wealth of this increasing number of institutions is shrinking, either. Gross national spending on higher education has gone from $12 billion in 1950 to $53 billion in 1965 to over $100 billion today. The wealth—the endowments—of our institutions of higher education has also continued to increase, especially in the past few years.

But to say this is to adopt a false criterion of well-being for our institutions of higher education, a criterion their spokesmen too often adopt. It is to mistake a means for an end. Now, I work in Washington, and I see higher education much of the time through its representatives there. Of those representatives I would say this: I have never seen a greater interest in *money* among anybody. These higher education lobbyists put Harvard Square hawkers to shame. They are, admittedly, very good at getting their funds from a Congress seemingly cowed by the pieties, pontifications, and poor-mouthings of American higher education. But very few words can be heard from any of these representatives about other aspects of higher education—issues like purpose, quality, curriculum, the moral authority and responsibilities of universities; most of the time, all we hear from them are pleas for money, for more money.

For example, recently the American Council on Education appointed a thirty-three-member national Commission on National Challenges in Higher Education; the purpose is to provide "a new, exciting agenda" for higher education. But this agenda is limited in an interesting way: the commission will *not* deal with such issues as what should be taught or what students are learning. Rather, the president of the ACE said, "We will be looking at such questions as 'What does higher education mean . . . to the people who fund us?' and 'What are their responsibilities?' " Notice: *their* responsibilities. And the purpose of the exercise, it is reported, is that "it is hoped that, by highlighting the importance of education to the nation, the Commission can coax additional funds from Congress." Is it likely that this report will be an examination of the real national challenges in higher education?

Even supporters of increased government spending on higher education are coming to find the spectacle in Washington a bit much. Thus the *Washington Post* recently took issue with colleges' objections to the new tax bill, under the headline "Crying Towel for Colleges." And there is some danger that higher education's tendency to cry wolf so insistently and so tiresomely will lead even Congress, one of these days, to balk.

Money is a means. It can be used for good or ill. In some cases money has aided good things, but in others money has aided in a kind of corruption. Money has meant growth and expansion, which in some places has meant a diffusion and loss of focus, a loss of central purpose. And more money has given many in our universities the opportunity to avoid doing one thing above all—actually teaching large numbers of students; or, in some cases, any students. Bennett's axiom: After a certain point, the more money you have, the fewer distinguished professors you will have in the classroom. This is an oddity of academic life. X dollars buys the students one professor, $2x$ dollars buys them two, but $3x$ and $4x$ and

$5x$ dollars gradually remove the professor from the student, and $6x$ dollars may replace all the classroom professors with graduate students. So money is not an unambiguous good. In any case, it's often not that hard to get money—but to bring quality and focus and purpose, to a place, now that's harder.

My final topic is tolerance: the university as a home for the free exchange of ideas. We are all too familiar with recent incidents of denial of free speech on colleges campuses. As Wayne State University president David Adamany has said, "The whole nation knows that faculty members, students, academic administrators, and some governing boards have in recent years silenced unpopular speakers—especially speakers on the right. . . . The shame for those of us who are active liberals is that we do not join in a chorus of condemnation of our colleagues when right-leaning speakers are kept off of our campuses by threat or are silenced by disorder." Perhaps such a chorus of condemnation may now finally begin to be heard, and we will see the restoration of the American ideal of free expression.

And we should also be careful not to allow a more subtle and pervasive kind of conformism and intolerance to permeate our institutions of higher education. Let me put it simply. Prestigious, selective, leading universities—whatever modifier you wish—have a tendency in our time to show a liberal bias. This is partly because most of the people in the humanities and social sciences departments in these universities stand to the left of center. A 1984 Carnegie Foundation survey of the professoriate found that, among philosophy faculty at four-year institutions, 21.7 percent designated themselves as "left," *none* as "strongly conservative"; for the sociologists, the percentages were 37 percent versus 0.9 percent; for historians, 12.9 percent versus 3 percent. As teachers of the young, these professors may tend to tilt students in the direction of their own beliefs. (Also, many students coming to such universities think that a general liberal bias is expected of them.) So certain views are in a minority and, indeed, are unpopular.

This need not be a great problem, as long as we are very careful that a generally shared political viewpoint does not lead to the explicit or implicit censorship of unpopular ideas. Unpopular views—views unpopular in the academy, that is—should not merely be grudgingly tolerated there; they should be respected. Harvard professor James Q. Wilson wrote over a decade ago that of the five institutions of which he had been a part—the Catholic Church, the University of Redlands, the U.S. Navy, the University of Chicago, and Harvard University—it was Harvard that was perhaps the least open to free and uninhibited discussion. Combatting this sort of intolerance requires more than allowing an occasional dissenting outside speaker to appear on campus. It requires self-criticism and self-examination; it requires a conscious striving by the academy against the tendency to become home to a "herd of independent minds." For if you cannot hold or express or argue for an unorthodox view at a university without risk of penalty, either explicit penalty or social disdain, the university will collapse like a deck of cards, falling of its own weight. If we cannot protect the basic principle of academic freedom, then we cannot even begin to hope that our colleges and universities will evolve into a recognizable imitation of what they claim to be.

Universities deserve the kind of scrutiny they like to give to others. Universities cost a lot, and they puff and boast a lot. From time to time, it's not a bad idea to look at what's really going on, and to ask some hard questions. I hope that some in American higher education will take seriously the questions I've raised, and ask themselves how they can do better by their students—who are, after all, the purpose of the enterprise.

PART
FIVE

OUR
COMMON
CULTURE

SIXTEEN

The Young James Madison*

CHARACTER IS NOT cut in marble, solid and unalterable. It lives and changes and may become well or diseased as our bodies do, for character is a process and an unfolding. Men are always in the making, and both virtues and faults are capable of either shrinking or expanding. Sinners have a future, and saints have a past. So with James Madison, whose character and civic virtues shone perhaps even more brightly in his youth than later on. What jobs challenged the young Madison and brought forth the best in him? How were the character and civic values of the young Madison revealed in his special relation to books, to his education, to his friend Thomas Jefferson, to the cause and meaning of the American union and Constitution?

James Madison was born in 1751 in King George County, Virginia, and he began early in life to put together perhaps one of the most impressive résumés in American history. He entered the College of New Jersey at Princeton and received his Bachelor of Arts degree in 1771. From that point, Madison held a string of public offices: 1775, member of the Committee of Public Safety in Orange County, Virginia; 1776, a delegate to the new Virginia Revolutionary Convention at Williamsburg; 1777, member of the

* This chapter is based on a bicentennial lecture at the National Archives, Washington, D.C., October 16, 1986.

Virginia Council of State; 1781, delegate to the Continental Congress; member of the Virginia House of Delegates in 1785 when he wrote the brilliant *Memorial and Remonstrance* in favor of religious liberty. In 1787, as one chronology, my favorite one for its terseness, puts it, he "drew up outline of new system of government," and in 1787–88 "contributed to *The Federalist* papers, and successfully led pro-constitutional debate in Virginia convention." It was in this period, 1775–88, that Madison's remarkable character became manifest.

Madison was a young intellectual whose passion was politics and a young politician whose passion was ideas. This combination has not been appreciated by all. On one side, many modern-day writers in political theory simply ignore him. On the other, it is thought, as Patrick Henry once put it, that "Madison is a theoretic statesman." This was said with contempt. It might still evoke the contempt of some in Washington today.

Indeed, Madison had a special relationship to learning. The James Madison Memorial Building of the Library of Congress would, I think, please him, for he would be happy to be so closely associated with books. To Madison, many things were unnecessary, but books were indispensable. It is said that he always read, and more, that he always read for a purpose. He knew there was an intimate connection between books and politics; in his bones he knew, and embodied, the intimate relation between what citizens read and what animates public life. Specifically, he believed that schemes, plans, and designs of government which one did not study or which one alone could not think of, were schemes, plans and designs that one was neither free to have for onself, nor to give to one's descendants. So books mattered: they contained all these things. A man is not free to plan and design what he has not learned or thought of.

Madison was the moving force behind the 1783 recommendation of "a list of books proper for the use of Congress," an idea eventually culminating in the Library of Congress. What he recommended was a guide to the ideal legislator's library: the works of Locke, Hooker, Plutarch, Hobbes, Hume, Montesquieu, Machiavelli, Plato, Aristotle, to name a few. The idea is clear. But we must go back even further, to the Madison of elementary and secondary school age, because Madison began reading good books when he was very young, before he ever saw Princeton. On his own, this frail little boy studied Greek, Latin, French, Spanish, and mathematics; he was taken by the moral force of Addison and Steele's *Spectator,* which he devoured. When he went to Princeton, he was already well educated and at Princeton he continued to read.

At the College of New Jersey at that time, there were other stimuli in addition to books. Overseeing the curriculum and all the students at Princeton was the famous Scottish-born divine, the feared and fearsome Dr. John Witherspoon. As president of the college in a now almost universally superannuated practice, Witherspoon lectured in moral philosophy to all his students.

Witherspoon taught Madison and Philip Freneau and William Bradford and the others, Madison's friends, a great number of things, but most of his lectures could be subsumed under one steady and constant Witherspoonian exhortation: "Do not live useless and die contemptible." Unlike many in today's schools, Witherspoon didn't worry that he was imposing his values on students. Stimulated by Witherspoon's intellect, Madison's mind bloomed.

So Madison studied. He remained an extra year at the college in preparation for a career in public life, where he did not study public policy, opinion polls, or behavioral trends, but Hebrew and ethics, history and theology. So at Princeton, as the historian Douglas Adair says, "the arguments of the philosophers became for Madison the slogans of a fighting faith and a political career."

What else did Madison get out of college? He succeeded in acquiring that to which many good students are entitled, that mixed blessing and curse in which a good college education plays a part: that is, right after college, and partly because of it, young James suffered an identity crisis. But from his college education he also found the means to get out of it. We see him, at the age of twenty-two, returning to Virginia and writing to Billy Bradford that he did not expect a long or healthy or productive life. "As to myself," he wrote, "I am too dull and infirm now to look out for any extraordinary things in this world, for I think my sensations for many months past have intimated to me not to expect a long and healthy life. I have little spirit or elasticity to set about anything that is difficult in acquiring." Madison was one of that

breed of very good students known to any teacher—the fine undergraduate who underrates himself.

But with the support and encouragement of friends, Madison
read and read and worked and worked and wrote and wrote, and
he put his young life together. So when he arrived in Philadelphia
in 1787, twelve days early for the Constitutional Convention, he
was the best prepared of all the members on the issues before it.
But this wasn't unusual for this man who loved the action and
passion of his times and who loved books. He was always prepared; he always did his homework.

Now began the vital center of Madison's career as a theoretic
statesman. His own efforts and the times were now to thrust greatness upon him. He had just the character and ability that were
needed by his country, that were to become a national resource.
Let's look first at Madison's character as politician.

Madison's special relation to politics can be simply described:
he loved politics. In politics, in the old politics of the smoke-filled
rooms at Philadelphia, situations were always unfolding but were
seldom fully unfolded. But this bright young man could see where
they were going and more than once he made both his classical
learning and his quick intelligence count, and count in the nick
of time. As Professor T. V. Smith says, Madison was that rarity: an
intellectual who understood, and loved, both politics and state-
craft. Ortega y Gasset says in *The Revolt of the Masses,* "Politics is
made up of unique situations in which a man suddenly finds himself submerged whether he will or no. Hence, politics is a test,
which allows us better to distinguish who are the clear heads and
who are the routiners." More than once Madison made it evident
that he was one of the clear heads.

For example, early in the federal convention, Roger Sherman
of Connecticut argued that the objects of union, of the new government, must be very few. They should be limited, he said, to
defense against foreign danger, to protection against internal disputes and the resort to force, and to needed treaties. Sherman, no
fool and not alone, was for giving the government power to legislate and execute only within a sharply defined province. Madison
was quick to his feet. To paraphrase the record: Mr. Madison
differed from Mr. Sherman in thinking the objects mentioned to

be all the principal ones that required a national government. Those the gentleman from Connecticut mentioned were certainly important and necessary, but Mr. Madison combined with them the necessity of providing more effectually for the security of private rights and the steady dispensation of justice. For it was interferences with these that, perhaps more than anything else, produced this convention. Was it to be supposed, Mr. Madison said, that republican liberty could long exist under the abuses of it practiced in some of the states? Mr. Sherman had to admit that in a very small state faction and oppression would prevail. With this admission, Madison moved in and, as the record says, argued: "Were we not then admonished to enlarge the sphere as far as the nature of the government would admit? This is the only defense against the inconveniences of democracy consistent with the democratic form of government." Though Madison's view was further debated and qualified, he, with his fellow Virginians, had set the terms of discussion.

But Madison didn't always win; he wasn't always successful. He frequently lost; he lost on his (original) opposition to a bill of rights. Madison was certainly not opposed to rights, but he feared, this theoretic statesman, what many thoughtful persons and sensible administrators fear: that enumeration would mean delimitation. He wrote to Jefferson in 1788: "There is great reason to fear that a positive declaration of some of the most essential rights could not be obtained in the requisite latitude. I am sure that the rights of conscience in particular, if submitted to public definition, would be narrowed much more than they are likely ever to be by an assumed power." In Madison's mind it was not the state that gave rights. If in enumeration they missed one, it might be lost forever or taken to be a dispensation from the state for which a sovereign people would have to beg. Finally, on this issue, Madison showed that he could change his mind, and he did.

He lost at the Convention on other matters. He lost on his wish for a federal veto on legislation in the states; he lost on proportional representation for the Senate as well as the House; he lost on his desire to abolish the slave trade immediately or at most in a few years.

But overall, on balance, he won. Now how did he take it?

You find out about a man and his character in defeat and in victory. Both in defeat and victory Madison revealed a steady equanimity, he maintained an even quality of sportsmanship. He was able to prepare himself for occasional defeat without becoming defeatist. When he lost, he put it behind him. His communication with others—friend and opponent—was frank, quick, manly. And his sense of sportsmanship gave him patience; he had the gift of the superb politician, the tactic, as Professor Smith calls it, of "creative waiting."

Now, politics involves compromise. Was Madison, the theoretic statesman, willing to compromise? Duff Cooper, the biographer of Talleyrand, has said of compromise that there is a great difference between the willingness on principle to compromise—a willingness Madison, given the respect he had for his colleagues, had in abundance—and the willingness to compromise on principles. Properly, Madison had no such willingness of the second sort. The federal union was his object, and when he lost on subsidiary matters, as long as he did not lose on that which mattered most, he took it in stride. He didn't curse his opponents (or if he did so, apparently he did it privately, out of earshot of his colleagues), but returned to the business at hand.

Perhaps he was able to do all this with equanimity because he resisted the seductive appeal of the absolute. He never worked for the absolute, but for the better; he did not make the political good the hostage of the best. He took the eventual prohibition of the slave trade when he could not get the immediate prohibition, but he did what he could to stretch the possible from the better to the much better. And finally, Madison knew, as Tommy Corcoran said, that you can't take the politics out of politics. And Madison loved politics.

Books and politics were not all that he loved. There was a well-developed social and personal side, too. He was said to be entertaining at parties—not a lampshade-on-the-head jester, but he was witty, liked a good joke, and could take one. It was said that he told good, colorful stories. But I think the most memorable part of the personal Madison was Madison as a friend, and particularly as a friend of Thomas Jefferson. For Madison's friendship with Jefferson was an embodiment of that kind of perfect friendship that Aristotle describes. It included pleasure and utility, but over and above that there was a shared purpose, a common end, and an enduring goodness on both sides.

It was so fine a friendship that more than one of Madison's biographers has asked whether there was ever a friendship comparable to that between Jefferson and Madison in intimacy, in duration (it lasted more than fifty years), in the degree of collaboration—and in the truthfulness of that collaboration. It's hard to think of many competitors. Perhaps, as some have suggested, justice can be done to it only by recalling another friendship: "And the soul of Jonathan was knit with the soul of David, and Jonathan loved him as his own soul." Madison and Jefferson met— could it have been in any other year?—in 1776 and worked together, starting then, on all aspects of revolutionary efficiency and later on the new scheme of government.

But they were different. Jefferson was a visionary and a philosopher, if not in the strict sense, he was at least an intellectual. Yet for all his closeness to philosophy, his was a mind guided less by the wisdom of the past than by its own flashing, creative, often idiosyncratic luminosity. The revolution in the young country needed such a mind: the song had to be sung, the Declaration had to ring in men's ears.

But the country also needed—and Jefferson needed—a companion who could consistently translate republican ideals into political institutions, someone who could test the ringing principle against its various applications. So Madison's analyses were the litmus for Jefferson's visions. For example, "the earth belongs to the living," Jefferson pronounced in a famous phrase, and let each generation of the living make their own laws. Well, this may sound good, but could it survive scrutiny? No, said James Madison. James Madison, the theoretic statesman, pointed out that if the earth belongs to the living and the living are free to legislate the past out of existence, then there will be serious problems: the danger of interregnum; periodic revisions in the laws that would encourage pernicious factions, and, he asked, "if the earth belongs to the living," what of laws, what of rules concerning the descent of estates and inheritances? Should such be in the hands of the living? If so, what a mess. And finally, Madison said to Jefferson that a continuously novel government loses the sanction of tradition and ultimately the "cumulative respect of a patriotic citizenry." The young James Madison could parse, do the syntax of, a principle as well as any man then or since. He was the ally Jefferson needed.

The intellectual differences between Jefferson and Madison were mirrored in their physical and temperamental differences. Jefferson was striking, a natural aristocrat, tall and rangy—six foot two—stylish, even modish in dress. But Madison was nature's commoner, small—five foot four—barely 100 pounds (it was once said that he looked like a withered little apple), dressed always in gray or black, meagerly equipped for a heroic role—indeed, as one commentator put it, ill-equipped for a hero's role in every natural attribute but intelligence. Jefferson was not averse to being in the center of things, or to having it known that he was in the center of things—though it is true that he often wished to be at home reading. Madison, too, was in the center of things. He did have, as one contemporary put it, a kind of chronic presence—but Madison had, and sought, a kind of chronic anonymity. Unlike Jefferson, history has more or less given it to him.

Perhaps this is a bit whimsical, but I regard another difference as interesting between these two men. Where was the center, the heart? What was the ordering of the *ordo amoris*? May we infer anything from the things they loved?

Jefferson loved books, and he loved Virginia, and he loved France. When we think of Jefferson, it is easy to think of him in Virginia, in the house at Monticello, or in Paris. And in some ways, I think he was a man of both Virginia and of France. But James Madison cannot be thought of in any other land but this. Madison never left America, and perhaps this was because of the unreliability of his health, as he himself said. But perhaps instead it was, as one scholar has put it, because he was in and of Virginia and America so completely that the need for European experience did not exist in him. Jefferson loved Paris, its commerce in fashion as well as its commerce in ideas. "Here in France," Jefferson once wrote John Adams, "it seems that a man might pass a life without encountering a single rudeness. Were I to proceed to tell you how much I enjoy their architecture, sculpture, painting, music, I should want words." Well, Adams' response is less cordial than Madison's might have been, but it echoed something of what would have been Madison's sentiment. For Adams, that hearty republican, after reading Jefferson's letter about the glories of France—painting, music, no rudeness—wrote back to him: "But what is this to me? I receive but little pleasure in beholding all these things because I cannot but consider them as bagatelles introduced by time and luxury in exchange for the hardy, manly virtues of the human heart." Madison, no less than Adams, did not share in the same measure of long-lasting enthusiasm Jefferson had for the French Revolution. So it was of Madison, not Jefferson, that James Barbour of Virginia said, "Is not in him the good genius of his country personified?"

A final word about Madison and Jefferson's friendship. Four and a half months before he died, when he was ailing, debt-ridden, and worried about his impoverished family, Jefferson confided this to his old friend:

> The friendship which has subsisted between us, now half a century, and the harmony of our political principles and pursuits, have been sources of constant happiness to me through that long period. . . . It has also been a great solace to me, to believe that you are engaged in vindicating to posterity the course we have pursued for preserving to them, in all their purity, the blessings of self-government, which we had assisted too in acquiring for them. If ever the earth had beheld a system of administration conducted with a single and steadfast eye to the general interest and happiness of those committed to it, one which, protected by truth, can never know reproach, it is that to which our lives have been devoted. To myself you have been a pillar of support through life. Take care of me when dead, and be assured that I shall leave with you my last affections.

A week later Madison replied:

> You cannot look back to the long period of our private friendship and political harmony, with more affecting recollections than I do. If they are a source of pleasure to you, what ought they not be to me? We cannot be deprived of the happy consciousness of the pure devotion to the public good, with which we discharged the trusts committed to us. And I indulge a confidence that sufficient evidence will find its way to another generation, to ensure, after we are gone, whatever of justice may be withheld whilst we are here.

I wonder if there has ever been a friendship of greater public consequence than that of Thomas Jefferson and James Madison.

Madison was not without fears for the new nation. In one of the most frequently quoted passages of *The Federalist*, the young Madison speaks of the danger of faction. A faction, he says in part, is a group of citizens united by "some common impulse of passion, or of interest, adverse to the rights of other citizens, or to the permanent and aggregate interests of the community." It is inevitable, he knew, that factions will arise in a free society; for "liberty is to faction as air is to fire." Yet the liberty that made factions possible also encouraged great virtue. If we look at the career of the young James Madison, his partiality and interest were ever selflessly focused on the same cause: republican government and union. To him that cause was the aim. Most else was expendable, including the credit for its founding.

Madison's commitment to union was so complete, so deep, that he was able in an extraordinary way to anticipate and describe not only the desired structure of that union but also a sense of its "pulse." A government, like a society, like any institution—a company, a team, a college—has not only its structure, its laws, its lore; it has a feel, a mood, a pulse.

We can discern the feel of what Madison sought in many of his writings. Consider the following example: One of the problems facing the first Congress was the question of titles; this was an important matter of tone for a new country. What, for example, should the chief executive be called? It was hoped that he would be given a title with the requisite authority and dignity so that he would be respected as the king had been formerly. Yet, obviously, there were fears that things could go too far in this direction. John Adams and a committee of friends had suggested "His Highness, President of the United States and Protector of the Rights of the Same." For this suggestion, Adams received much ridicule. "Mr. Adams and the men from Massachusetts," one sarcastic commentator wrote, "have misunderstood the revolution; they want the loaves and fishes of government and wish to transfer the scepter from London to Boston."

On May 11, 1788, Madison rose in Congress to speak against royalist-sounding titles. Though not regarded as one of Madison's most critical addresses, it's a telling one. He said:

I am not afraid of titles because I fear the danger of any power they could confer, but I am against them because they are not very reconcilable with the nature of our government or the genius of our people. Even if they were proper in themselves, they are not so at this juncture of time. But my objection is founded in principle; instead of increasing, they diminish the true dignity and importance of a republic and would in particular, on this occasion, diminish the dignity of the first magistrate himself. If we borrow, the servile imitation will be odious, not to say ridiculous also; for we must copy from the pompous sovereigns of the East or follow the inferior potentates of Europe. In either case the splendid tinsel or gorgeous robe would disgrace the manly shoulders of our chief. The more truly honorable shall we be by showing a total disregard and neglect to things of this nature. The more simple, the more republican we are in our manners the more rational dignity we shall acquire.

Rational dignity, simple republican manners—here's the pulse. In Madison indeed was the "good genius of his country personified."

William James wrote that the great use of a life is to spend it for something that outlasts it. Madison and his colleagues gave us a working blueprint that still has a magnificent vitality. As James Bryce said in *The American Commonwealth*, the world watches with more than a little interest how this experiment will turn out. Unlike other nations, we have lived long and continuously, with only small emendations, under a single document. It is different elsewhere. (I am reminded of the story of the nineteenth-century Englishman who went to the library and asked the clerk for a copy of the French Constitution. "I'm sorry, sir," said the clerk, "we don't keep periodicals here.") Our blueprint is not a utopian one, "not a plan based on the deceitful dream of a golden age," not a plan for a New Man, but something better. "We are teaching the world the great lesson that men do better without kings and nobles than with them," Madison wrote. And at bottom, of course, the plan was made of ideas, the outcome of a long intellectual inheritance. Madison did not invent the theory of the rights of man or the purposes of government. He was not a systematic philosopher. But through him, this theoretic statesman, with a degree of intentionality and foresight not seen before or since, these ideas were galvanized into the fabric of our nation.

There may not be a better case study of the truth that ideas matter, that ideas have consequences, than the tracing of Madison's intellectual/political career. These ideas, his ideas, mattered. Different ideas shape social fabrics, different societies are formed. And the differences are seen today. It matters whether one follows the ideas of a Madison or the ideas of a Marx.

The ideas of James Madison which helped make a nation also have gone far toward defining who we are as a people. On this point, John Quincy Adams said it best. Speaking in Congress shortly after Madison's death, Adams said: "Is it not in a pre-eminent degree by emanations from his mind that we are assembled here as the representatives of the people and the states of this Union? Is it not transcendentally by his exertions that we address each other here by the endearing appellation of country-men and fellow-citizens?"

SEVENTEEN

A Plea for History*

MY TOPIC HERE is history and citizenship—a plea for the teaching of the first for the sake of the second. In 1892 the National Education Association created the now-famous Committee of Ten to study ways of developing good citizenship in the schools. Chaired by Harvard president Charles Eliot and composed of distinguished educators (including five college presidents), the committee recommended an eight-year course in history from fifth through twelfth grades. Students in the fifth and sixth grades would begin with biography and mythology. American history and government would be taught in the seventh grade; Greek and Roman history in the eighth grade; French history (as an illustration of European history in general) in the ninth grade; English history (because of its contribution to American institutions) in the tenth grade; American history in the eleventh grade; and there would be an intensive study of a special historical topic in the twelfth grade.

In making these recommendations, the Committee of Ten echoed Thomas Jefferson's views on the importance of historical knowledge. In 1816, Jefferson had written:

* This chapter is based on the Alf Landon Lecture, Kansas State University, Manhattan, Kansas, September 9, 1986.

History, by apprizing [Americans] of the past, will enable them to judge of the future; it will avail them of the experience of other times and other nations; it will qualify them as judges of the actions and designs of men; it will enable them to know ambition under every disguise it may assume; and knowing it, to defeat its views.

The Committee of Ten asserted that when historical studies are taught in conjunction with literature, geography, and foreign languages, they "serve to broaden and cultivate the mind . . . they counteract a narrow and provincial spirit . . . they prepare the pupil in an eminent degree for enlightened and intellectual enjoyment in after years" and "they assist him to exercise a salutary influence upon the affairs of his country."

Several years later, another NEA report endorsed these views. History, it argued, was "peculiarly appropriate in a secondary course, which is fashioned with the thought of preparing boys and girls for the duties of daily life and intelligent citizenship." As a direct result of these reports, by 1915 the overwhelming majority of American high schools offered courses in ancient history, medieval and modern history, English history and American history.

Given this unanimity on the importance of the study of history for democratic citizenship, one might reasonably expect that contemporary American students would be fairly well versed in the essentials of American and world history. Unfortunately, this is not the case. As Professor Paul Gagnon of the University of Massachusetts has written:

Today many of our freshmen arrive at college, after twelve years of school (presumably in the "college track"), knowing nothing of the pre-Plymouth past, including the Bible! All too frequently, they have not heard of Aristotle, Aquinas, Luther, Machiavelli, Hobbes, Locke, Montesquieu, Burke, or Marx. They often know nothing of the deterioration of Athens and Rome, of Czarist Russia and Weimar Germany, and next to nothing of the history of science, technology, industry, of capitalism and socialism, of fascism and Stalinism, of how we found ourselves in two world wars, or even in Vietnam. They have been asked to read very little and to reflect hardly at all. At eighteen or nineteen, they are unarmed for public discourse, their great energy and idealism at the mercy of pop politics and the seven o'clock news.

Professor Gagnon's conclusions are borne out by a number of recent studies. For example, a 1986 survey by the National Assessment of Educational Progress revealed that eleventh graders know astonishingly little about American history. Two-thirds could not place the Civil War within the period 1850–1900; one-third did not know that the Declaration of Independence was signed between 1750 and 1800; one-third did not know that Columbus sailed before 1750; half could not locate the half-century in which World War I occurred; half did not recognize the names Winston Churchill and Joseph Stalin.

Equally distressing is the widespread ignorance of history's sister discipline, geography. Ninety-five percent of the university students in North Carolina failed a basic geography test administered in 1985. Among the questions asked: What was the approximate 1980 population of the United States? What are the two largest states in area? In what countries are Baghdad, Lisbon, Madras, Manila, Capetown, and Budapest located? Many of our college students, it seems, think Canada is a state. Most cannot find Israel on a map.

The point is clear. Our young people are woefully ill-educated about the history and basic principles of our nation and our civilization. For those who believe, with Thomas Jefferson, that a knowledge of history belongs at the very center of every American's "general education," this lack of knowledge is cause for alarm.

How did it happen? Why don't our students have an adequate grasp of history and geography? Our children did not suddenly become more ignorant. They certainly did not choose to become more ignorant. It is not *their* fault. The answer has to do with changing intellectual fashions in the field of education—fashions that affected adults, and that led adults to fail to teach our children what they should know.

Some twenty-five years after the Committee of Ten published its report on the importance of history, the NEA issued yet another report, known as *The Cardinal Principles of Secondary Education*. This is generally considered the single most important document in the history of American education. What is perhaps most noteworthy about it is its claim that the major purpose of modern education is to promote what it called "social efficiency." The promotion of social efficiency meant that "facts, conditions, theories and activities that do not contribute rather directly to the appreciation of methods of human betterment have no claim" on the overwhelming majority of high school students. And included among these "facts, conditions and theories" was the study of history. For how, after all, could history contribute "rather directly" to human betterment? It didn't improve anyone's health; it didn't make anyone a better worker; it didn't teach adolescents how to behave on a date or find a job. Thus, as Professor Diane Ravitch points out, "In the new era of social efficiency and pupil interests, the year-long course on ancient history began to disappear from American schools, and before long the four-year history sequence was telescoped to three, then to two, and, in many places, to only a single year of American history."

Today, even the very subject of history is in danger of losing its distinct identity, of becoming absorbed in the smorgasbord of this and that known as "social studies." And, as the Council for Basic Education wrote in its 1982 report, *Making History Come Alive,* "parents are likely to presume that if their children are taking any social studies courses, they are learning history. They may or may not be."

The Council for Basic Education report largely confirmed the findings of a 1975 study conducted by the Organization of American Historians. The OAH study noted a significant decline in the teaching of secondary school history throughout the country. It found that in some states "virtually no training in history is demanded" of secondary school teachers. In one state, history teachers were being encouraged to emphasize concepts that transcend "any given historical situation." In another state, the trend was toward ethnocultural courses; in another, the focus was on problem solving, decision making, and social action. And in another, the OAH predicted that history would be supplanted by more "relevant" courses such as consumer affairs, ecology, and multicultural studies.

Fortunately, there are now efforts under way to restore history to the school curriculum. In California, for example, the state superintendent of schools Bill Honig, has been effective in persuading educators to adopt more demanding course requirements. But if these and other efforts are to bear fruit, we must have a clear idea about history's importance, about what the study of history can and cannot accomplish. In what way does the study of history contribute to our betterment? What subjects should our children study in their history courses and why should they study them?

Intellectual honesty requires us to concede at the outset that history has little practical utility comparable to the physical sciences. As the great British historian George Macaulay Trevelyan wrote in 1913, "No one can by a knowledge of history, however profound, invent the steam engine, or light a town, or cure cancer, or make wheat grow near the arctic circle." Moreover, although historians from Polybius to Toynbee have tried to deduce general laws of "cause and effect" in human affairs comparable to the laws of physical science, all such attempts have failed. For, to quote Trevelyan once again, "the law of gravitation may be scientifically proved because it is universal and simple. But the historical law that starvation brings on revolt is not proved; indeed the opposite statement, that starvation leads to abject submission, is equally true in the light of past events. You cannot so completely isolate any historical event from its circumstances as to be able to deduce from it a law of general application. Only politicians adorning their speeches with historical arguments have this power; and even they never agree." While Trevelyan argued that history could never be made "scientific," he insisted, nonetheless, on its centrality. Why?

We'll consider an example from a turbulent era in our own history. The passage of the Kansas-Nebraska Act of 1854 set off a wave of violence in "bloody Kansas" between abolitionists and pro-slavers. What manner of men were the abolitionists? A number of perfectly respectable historians have branded them as "extremists," "impractical," "trouble-makers," and "not free of racial prejudice themselves." Other historians, equally respectable, have defended the abolitionists as "men of conscience," "courageous," and "Christian." As it is not likely that this controversy will ever be definitively resolved, the only way that a student can arrive at a useful judgment about the abolitionists is by reading different historians, by reading the actual words of the abolitionists and their critics, by being exposed to conflicting points of view, and then by thinking out the problem for himself. And in the process of thinking things out, of weighing the facts and searching for the truth, he acquires a respect for facts and for the proper methods of weighing evidence. He learns to distinguish superficiality from depth, bias from objectivity, tendentiousness from honesty, stupidity from discernment, and confusion from lucidity. In short, he acquires what is surely one of the most important skills of democratic citizenship: the ability to think critically about society and its affairs.

But for the study of history to have this educative effect, it must not be taught simply as an accumulation of received truths, dead facts, and dry figures. It should stimulate a series of questions that we can put to the past, then attempt to relate the answers in the context of the present day. In this way, we find meaning in the world and insight into what other people have made of their lives.

A gifted teacher of history is not only someone who encourages his or her students to develop their own powers of criticism, observation, and analysis. He or she is also someone who can convey the emotional and romantic aspect of history. As the American historian and literary critic Bernard De Voto has written, "If the mad, impossible voyage of Columbus or Cartier or La Salle or Coronado or John Ledyard is not romantic, if the stars did not dance in the sky when our Constitutional Convention met, if Atlantis has any landscape stranger or the other side of the moon any lights or colors or shapes more unearthly than the customary homespun of Lincoln and the morning coat of Jackson, well, I don't know what romance is. Ours is a story mad with the impossible; it began as dream and it has continued as dream down to the last headlines you read in a newspaper." In teaching American history, we must never lose sight of the fact that we are telling a story—sometimes a tragic tale, sometimes joyous, but always a great story, always a story "mad with the impossible."

Yet history is even more than a means of developing critical judgment, or an engrossing story. It is also an essential part of literacy. For literacy entails much more than recognizing the forms and sounds of words. It entails possessing a body of knowledge enabling us to make sense of the facts, names, and allusions cited by an author. In the words of University of Virginia professor E. D. Hirsch, literacy "turns out to be less a system of skills than a system of information"; the ability to comprehend depends chiefly on "the amount of relevant prior knowledge" one has. Literacy is content. It is knowledge.

The study of history is an incubator of critical intelligence, a tool of literacy, and a glorious entertainment. But history has yet another educative function, one which Leszek Kolakowski identified in his Jefferson Lecture in 1986 when he said that "we learn history . . . to know who we are"; it is to learn "why, and for what [we are] responsible" and how this responsibility is to be taken up. In other words, history is a source of personal identity, a means of acquiring a sense of "connectedness" with a tradition, a community, a past. It is a way of locating ourselves in time and space, of acquiring the values and ideals by which to live our lives, and of returning to the wellsprings of our being as a people and a nation. The current "erosion of a historically defined sense of 'belonging,'" Kolakowski warns, "plays havoc" with the lives of our young people and "threatens their ability to withstand possible trials of the future."

Acquiring a "historically defined sense of belonging" is especially important in the United States, for this nation was created in order to realize a specific political vision, and it is the memory of that political vision which defines us as Americans. Memory is the glue that holds our political community together, and history is organized memory. Only by studying American history, by celebrating its heroes anew in each generation, by understanding its failures as well as lauding its achievements, can students grasp the value of our political tradition.

Running through our nation's history like a golden thread are certain ideals and aspirations. We believe in liberty and justice and equality. We believe in limited government and in the betterment of the human condition. These truths underlie both our history and our society, and while they may be self-evident, they are not spontaneously apprehended by the young. They must be taught these things, and they should know that a large part of the world thinks and acts according to other principles.

Once we understand that history plays a central role in preparing our students for democratic citizenship, everything else falls into place. Thus, to help students appreciate the origins of democratic institutions and values, they must be taught something of the history of ancient Athens, of the Magna Carta, of revolutionary France, as well as of events in Philadelphia. In order to restore the place of history in our schools, specific curricular standards should be set by experts, and these should be carefully adhered to. And in order to acquaint younger children with their American heritage, we should not hesitate to draw on our nearly forgotten treasure trove of historical imagery and lore, on the exploits of Paul Bunyan and Johnny Appleseed, Daniel Boone and Benjamin Banneker.

Americans are heirs to a precious historical legacy. Let it never be said of us that we failed as a nation because we neglected to pass on this legacy to our children. Whatever our ancestry of blood, we are all equally heirs to the same tradition. In one sense we all have the same fathers—our Founding Fathers. Let it be said that we told our children their story, and the whole story, the long record of our glories, of our failures, of our aspirations, our sins, our achievements and our victories. Then let us leave them to determine their own view of it all: America in the totality of its acts. If we can dedicate ourselves to that endeavor, I am confident that our students will discern in the story of their past the truth. And they will cherish that truth. And it will keep them free.

EIGHTEEN

Religious Belief and the Constitutional Order *

I WILL FOCUS here not on constitutional law but on constitutional principles—on the moral and philosophical underpinnings of the document at the base of our republic. I have studied the Constitution as a student of philosophy and as a student of law. So I am confident when I say that it's time to retrieve the Constitution from the lawyers. For the Constitution belongs to all of us. It was written not only to protect our legal rights but also to express our common values. And we cannot understand ourselves as individuals without understanding the ideas that "constitute" us as a people.

As the emblem of our national values, the Constitution reflects three distinct but related elements of our common culture: the Judeo-Christian ethic, the democratic ethic, and the work ethic. In fact, the process that produced the Constitution has itself been ascribed to all three of these ethics. To Walt Whitman, the Constitution was a "bible of the free" for the modern world. To John Quincy Adams, the Constitution was the product of democratic compromise. He said that it was "extorted from the grinding necessity of a reluctant nation." To William Gladstone, the Constitution was the product of hard work. He called it "the greatest work

* This chapter is based on the Paine Lecture, University of Missouri, Columbia, Missouri, September 17, 1986.

ever struck off at a given time by the brain and purpose of man." Of these three aspects of our constitutional order, I will address myself to the first: the role of religion and the Judeo-Christian ethic in American democracy.

I am in sympathy with the religious beliefs of the overwhelming majority of the American people—although I am personally, I would guess, rather average in the degree of my religious observance. But my upbringing, my experience, and my studies have made me sympathetic to religious beliefs. In my encounters with the academic community, I am often struck by the fact that, of all the issues I address, my support of religion seems to inspire the deepest bewilderment and suspicion.

Of course, it is not only members of the academy who disagree with me. In 1985 I gave a speech to the Knights of Columbus on the relationship of our political and social order to religious belief. I stated my position clearly: that the American experience cannot be understood without reference to the Judeo-Christian tradition, and that the First Amendment was not intended to result in the complete exclusion of that tradition from public life. For saying this, I was attacked as an "Ayatollah." It was suggested that merely broaching the subject of religion in public life was an incitement to "Khomeinism." It was also suggested that I considered myself a messenger "heaven-sent to silence the heathen."

I have described this line of attack as a *reductio ad Khomeini*. It ignores my reaffirmation in that speech of this nation's commitment to the principles of tolerance and equal rights for all—for the nonbeliever as well as for the believer. With its fear of religious intolerance, the attack denies the fundamental strength of the American people—a people at once deeply religious and deeply tolerant. And the attack betrays a misconception that it is somehow improper for public officials to speak publicly and positively about the role of religion in American life.

The Founders discussed the role of religion in democracy calmly and frankly. Let us follow their lead and reclaim their legacy. There are those who argue that it is impossible, in the twentieth century, to gauge the intent of the Founders in the eighteenth century. I disagree. On the question of religion and the Constitution, the Framers' intent is explicit and history is clear. It is true that the Framers were themselves divided by a rich diversity of religious allegiances and personal convictions. But virtually all were united by a common belief in the importance of religion as an aid and a friend to the constitutional order. As Alexis de Tocqueville said, "I do not know whether all Americans have a sincere faith in their religion—for who can search the human heart?—but I am certain that they hold it to be indispensable to the maintenance of republican institutions."

From devout churchgoers to rationalizing deists, the Founders spoke with one voice about the importance of including religion in civic life. Washington, a Virginia Episcopalian, warned in his Farewell Address: "Of all the dispositions and habits which lead to political prosperity, religion and morality are indispensable supports. . . . And let us with caution indulge the supposition that morality can be maintained without religion." John Adams, a Massachusetts Unitarian, agreed in no uncertain terms: "Our Constitution was made only for a moral and religious people. It is wholly inadequate to the government of any other." Madison, another Episcopalian, insisted that "before any man can be considered as a member of Civil Society, he must be considered as a subject of the Governor of the Universe." And even Jefferson agreed. Jefferson, the great deist who was always skeptical of sectarianism in any form, asked, "Can the liberties of a nation be thought secure when we have removed their only firm basis, a conviction in the minds of the people that these liberties are the gift of God?" Religion, he concluded, should be regarded as "a supplement to law in the government of men," and as "the alpha and omega of the moral law."

I could go on, quoting source after source, speech after speech. From Sam Adams to Patrick Henry to Benjamin Franklin to Alexander Hamilton, all of the Founders intended religion to provide a moral anchor for our liberty in democracy. Yet all would be puzzled were they to return to America today. For they would find, among certain elite circles in the academy and in the media, a fastidious disdain for the public expression of religious values—a disdain that clashes directly with the Founders' vision of religion as a friend of civic life. That is why it is not enough merely to identify the intent of the Founders. It is also necessary to *defend* the intent of the Founders.

The first question we should ask ourselves is: Why did the

Founders see a connection between religious values and political liberty? Tocqueville points to an answer. "Liberty regards religion . . . as the safeguard of morality, and morality as the best security of law and the surest pledge of the duration of freedom." In short, Tocqueville concluded, religion "is more needed in democratic republics than in any others."

But it is not necessary to go back to Tocqueville to see the connections between religion and liberty in democracy. It's simply common sense: our commitment to liberty of conscience—including the freedom to believe or not to believe—follows, in good part, from the respect for religion felt by the majority of Americans. It is ironic that anyone who appeals today to religious values runs the risk of being called "divisive" or attacked as an enemy of pluralism. For the readiness of most Americans to defend tolerance and equality does not derive only from an abstract allegiance to Enlightenment ideals. It comes also from a concrete allegiance to the Judeo-Christian ethic.

The connection between religion and liberty is one reason that the Founders considered religion to be indispensable to democracy. There are two more reasons. At its best, *religion deepens politics*. It is a wellspring of the civic virtues that democracy requires in order to flourish. It promotes hard work and individual responsibility. It lifts each citizen outside himself and inspires concern for community and country. It is a call to kindness and decency and forgiveness in our homes, our schools, and our communities. At the same time, it offers a sense of purpose and a frame of reference for claims that transcend everyday politics, such as our collective responsibility to foster liberty around the globe.

Religion promotes tolerance. This sounds like a paradox. Religion, after all, is about absolute truth, and does not the search for absolute truth lead to absolutism and *in*tolerance? Not necessarily—and in America, thankfully, not very often. As its most sectarian, religion can indeed be used in the service of intolerance. When religion is "kindled into enthusiasm," as Madison said, it may "become a motive to oppression as well as a restraint from injustice." But more often in America, religion has had the opposite effect. I am always struck by the way different schools receive me when I speak. I remember starting off a recent speech at a Baptist college—known for its fervor—by stipulating that I spoke as a Catholic. The audience was at first surprised by my frankness, but quickly settled down and courteously listened to what I had to say. Many even liked it. In this instance, strongly held religious convictions seemed to foster respect for the convictions of others. On the other hand, some in the so-called enlightened universities—aggressively secular, perhaps even intolerantly so—are more likely to greet me as an ayatollah and to shout down speakers with whom they disagree.

I think President Reagan put it well when he told an ecumenical prayer breakfast, "Our government needs the church because only those humble enough to admit they are sinners can bring to democracy the tolerance it requires in order to survive." I also think that the President's proposition cuts both ways. Just as religion moderates the potentially divisive tendencies of democracy, so a properly functioning democracy moderates the potentially divisive tendencies of religion. When religion is excluded from public life, it can become resentful, extremist, and sectarian. But when religion is included in public life and is subject to public scrutiny, it learns to speak in a language that all sects and all citizens can understand. As Jefferson wrote to Thomas Cooper, "By bringing the sects together . . . we shall soften their asperities, liberalize and neutralize their prejudices, and make the general religion a religion of peace, reason, and morality."

Jefferson was right. In a free democracy, where much depends on broad public sentiment, religious groups must indeed soften their asperities, and they find they must pursue their ends by appealing to a consensus of shared, not particularized, values. This has happened throughout American history, and it happens today.

The question of tolerance, moreover, points to a protection at the very heart of the Constitution: equal justice under law, for nonbelievers as well as believers. When Patrick Henry proposed "a moderate tax or contribution annually for the support of the Christian religion," Madison successfully opposed it on these grounds: "Whilst we assert for ourselves a freedom to . . . observe the Religion which we believe to be of divine origin, we cannot deny an equal freedom to those whose minds have not yet yielded to the evidence which has convinced us." And Jefferson agreed, in his Virginia statute for religious freedom: "No man," he said, "shall be compelled to frequent or support any religious worship place, or ministry whatsoever."

This is an important point. Absolute freedom of conscience is the first of our freedoms. The American people are irrevocably committed to equal rights for all. No one in America can be forced to assent to any particular religious belief, or even to the general religious beliefs derived from the Judeo-Christian tradition and embedded in our common culture. At the same time, however, religious beliefs do deserve acknowledgment, respect, and public encouragement. We tend to forget that the Founders saw no conflict between our individual rights and our common values. In their minds, complete neutrality between particular religious beliefs can and should coexist with public acknowledgment of general religious values.

This is not merely a question of constitutional principle, though it is that. It is also a question of civic health. My point is not simply that children who go to church are less likely to take drugs, or that empirical studies show an inverse relation between religious belief and teenage pregnancy, although both are true. My point is that we are coming to recognize the extent to which many of our social problems require for their solution the nurture and improvement of character. And for many of us, religion is an important part of the development of character. This is not to say that religious faith is necessary for sound character. But that it can help, and that it has helped many—who can doubt? And so, as we move toward a national consensus that, in dealing with social problems, we must improve the character of our citizenry, we should not, out of a misplaced fastidiousness, spurn the vast resources of ethical precept and practice that are inspired and reinforced by religious belief.

In effect, I am calling for a reconstitution of the consensus of the Founders. All of them were comfortable with a public role for religion, as long as there was no preference for one sect over another. To Jefferson, religion was an essential element of education. As the founder of the University of Virginia, Jefferson made provision for religious instruction with a "professor of ethics" rather than a clergyman. Students were required to take courses that taught the "moral obligations, of those in which all sects agree."

The early Congress, too, saw nothing unconstitutional about some support of religious values. The first three Congresses authorized chaplaincies for the Congress, the Army, and the Navy. And the same Congress that adopted the First Amendment also adopted the Northwest Ordinance, which reads: "Religion, morality, and knowledge being necessary to good government and the happiness of mankind, schools and the means of learning shall forever be encouraged." If Congress had meant to forbid all cooperation between the government and the church, why would it call on the states "to promote religious and moral education?" The Founders knew that it is never easy to maintain neutrality between sects. They knew that the preservation of equal rights requires political sensitivity and legal vigilance. But they also knew that, for the sake of liberty, government should acknowledge the religious beliefs on which democracy depends—not one single belief but belief in general.

History shows few other examples of nations that have managed to maintain the delicate balance between religious faith and political tolerance. In the twentieth century, we have seen both atheistic communism and religious fanaticism degenerate into tyranny. The Founding Fathers pledged their lives to avoid tyranny in any form. And the real genius of the Constitution lies in the balance it strikes between unity and diversity, between religious liberty and political equality, to the mutual benefit of both religion and politics.

But to maintain that balance is no easy task. In America today, we face misunderstandings from both ends of the spectrum—from the secularists on one side and from the sectarians on the other. First there is the secularist orthodoxy, which seeks to eradicate all signs of religion from public life. With a reckless disregard for both American history and the American people, some secularists are not content to pursue government neutrality among beliefs, or even government protection of nonbelief. They seek to vanquish religion altogether. For as former Supreme Court Justice Potter Stewart has pointed out, the banishment of religion does not represent neutrality between religion and secularism; the conduct of public institutions without any acknowledgment of religion is secularism.

In my opinion, the Supreme Court in recent years has failed

to reflect sufficiently on the relationship between our religious faith and our political order. The Court itself has acknowledged the lack of "clarity and predictability" in its decisions. But my purpose is not to criticize the Court; and the Court does not bear sole responsibility for the shunting aside of religion. A recent study by New York University professor Paul Vitz found that the overwhelming majority of elementary and high school textbooks go to extraordinary lengths to avoid any references to religion.

Here is a representative item from the study—just one among many. One sixth-grade reader includes a story called "Zlateh the Goat," by Nobel laureate Isaac Bashevis Singer. In the story, a boy named Aaron is told to take Zlateh, the family goat, to a butcher in the next village to be sold. On the way, Aaron and Zlateh get caught in a three-day blizzard and are lost in the snow. At this point, Singer writes, "Aaron began to pray to God for himself and for the innocent animal." But in the reader this has been changed to: "Aaron began to pray for himself and for the innocent animal." Later, after Aaron and Zlateh have found shelter in a haystack, Singer writes, "Thank God that in the hay it was not cold." But in the reader this has been changed to: "Thank goodness that in the hay it was not cold."

This would be funny if it were not so serious. Has the very mention of God's name in public become an offense? Among Orthodox Jews, it has always been considered a religious blasphemy to write the name of God in full. Well, have we come to the point where, in school textbooks, it is now considered a secular blasphemy to write the name of God, even if omitting His name does violence to the original text? Have we come to the point where it is now considered a secular blasphemy to acknowledge the name of God at all? Have we come, in some bizarre way, full circle, from scrupulous piety to fastidious disdain?

The main conclusion of Professor Vitz's study is that many high school textbooks go to extreme lengths to ignore the role of religion in American history. In case after case, the study points to exclusions, misrepresentations, and distortions, ranging from the silly to the outrageous. One world history book completely ignores the Reformation. An American history textbook defines pilgrims as "people who make long trips." Another defines fundamentalists as rural people who "follow the values or traditions of an earlier period." Still another lists three hundred important events in American history. Only three of the three hundred have anything to do with religion.

Soon after Professor Vitz's conclusions were released, Americans United for the Separation of Church and State conducted a study of its own. This is a group hardly sympathetic to the religious lobby. But it too agreed that "most high school social studies and civics textbooks completely ignore religious liberty and give little or no consideration to the religious clauses of the First Amendment." Then Norman Lear's People for the American Way acknowledged that state of affairs. Finally, the *Washington Post* published an op-ed piece called "A Liberal Case for Religion in School." We're making progress.

In 1749, Benjamin Franklin issued a set of "Proposals Relating to the Education of Youth in Pennsylvania." And he advocated, above all, the study of history, which would "afford frequent opportunities of showing the Necessity of a *Publick Religion,* from its Usefulness to the Publick; the Advantage of a Religious Character among private Persons; the Mischiefs of Superstitions, etc." Today, two centuries after the signing of the Constitution, let us remember Franklin and make a pledge to tell our children the truth, and the whole truth, about our history. The story of America is the story of the highest aspirations and proudest accomplishments of mankind. And it is impossible to understand those aspirations and accomplishments without understanding the religious roots from which they sprang. We should tell our children about the Puritans, who founded a "shining city" with a sacred mission: to be a beacon unto the nations and to lead a community of saints to the New Jerusalem. We should tell our children about Jefferson and Franklin, who proposed that the Great Seal of the United States depict Moses leading the chosen people from the wilderness to the promised land. We should tell our children about Abraham Lincoln, who saw the Civil War as "a punishment, inflicted upon us, for our presumptuous sins, to the needful end of our national reformation as a whole People." And we should tell our children about Reverend Martin Luther King, Jr., who carried the "gospel of freedom" to the mountaintop and who wrote a letter to the world from Birmingham Jail. "When these disinherited children of God sat down at lunch counters," he wrote, "they were in reality standing up for what is best in the American dream and for the most sacred values in our Judeo-Christian heritage."

In recent years, we have shown a reluctance to tell the whole truth. We have excluded religious history from our textbooks. We have excluded religious values from our public life. And we have paid a double price. First, our efforts to deny religious values in the name of religious liberty threaten the very toleration that it affirms. As John Locke reminds us: "Those that by their atheism undermine and destroy all religion can have no pretence of religion whereupon to challenge the privilege of a toleration." Second, we have created, in the words of Richard John Neuhaus, something like a "naked public square." We seem to be unable to celebrate in public the common values that most of us still affirm in private. And so our politics, deprived of religion, threaten to become short-sighted and self-interested. As we might expect, religion, excluded from politics, threatens to become resentful, extremist, and sectarian.

Ironically, those who seek to exclude religion from politics may end by inciting the dangers they fear. For there are some whose vision of America yields nothing in dogmatic certainty to the opposing vision of the secularists, and who, no less than the secularists, misunderstand the character of our constitutional order. There are some in America today who believe, like Samuel Adams, that America should be a "Christian Sparta." They properly deserve the name "sectarian" rather than "religious." For though they sometimes speak in the name of religion in general, they would promote their own particular brand of religion into a favored position in public life. Not content to bring religious values into the public square, they would deny the government's constitutional obligation to be neutral among particular religious communities.

Like their secular antagonists, these zealots suffer from a misreading of history. If the secularists assert, wrongly, that the Founders meant to exclude all public support of religion, then the sectarians assert, wrongly, that the Constitution was designed, first and foremost, "to perpetuate a Christian order." One scholar argues that Christianity was the primary cause of the American Revolution. He calls for a "Christian historiography and a Christian revisionism" to foster a "return to the Protestant restoration of feudalism." A newspaper columnist insists that the Founders intended that all schoolchildren be taught to acknowledge the divinity of Christ.

This is bad scholarship as well as dangerous politics. In the days of the Puritans, Massachusetts may indeed have been an intolerant Calvinist theocracy. But as the "church covenant" evolved into a "halfway covenant," so the Calvinist theocracy gave way to a constitutional democracy. By 1787 the Founders were determined at all costs to prevent the national government from establishing any form of religious orthodoxy. Throughout the last century, Protestants, Catholics, Jews, Buddhists, Muslims, and many others have flocked from all over the globe to the "shining city on a hill." All, in their turn, have come to find their own peace in this land of religious liberty.

On the one hand, religion should never be excluded from public debate. But on the other, it should never be used as a kind of divine trump card to foreclose further debate. Those who claim that their religious faith gives them a monopoly on political truth make democratic discourse difficult. Disagree with me and you're damned, they seem to suggest. In doing so, they insult the common sense and the tolerant spirit of the American people.

In America, the roots of religious liberty and political equality are long and deep. On August 17, 1790, in the first years of our constitutional government, the Hebrew Congregation of Newport, Rhode Island, wrote to President George Washington expressing thanks that the government of the United States gave "to bigotry no sanction, to persecution no assistance." This was the President's reply:

> The Citizens of the United States of America have a right to applaud themselves for having given to mankind examples of an enlarged and liberal policy; a policy worthy of imitation. All possess alike liberty of conscience and immunities of citizenship. It is now no more that toleration is spoken of, as if it was by the indulgence of one class of people, that another enjoyed the exercise of their inherent natural rights.

And Washington added, in beautiful words:

> May the Children of the Stock of Abraham, who dwell in this land, continue to merit and enjoy the good will of the other inhabitants, while every one shall sit in safety under his own vine and fig tree, and there shall be none to make him afraid.

So to those today who strike fear in others by calling America a "Christian nation," this is my reply: You are wrong. Sam Adams was wrong; we are not a "Christian Sparta." But Justice William Douglas was right when he said, "We are a religious people." We are indeed—the most religious free people on earth. A recent survey showed that while 76 percent of the British, 62 percent of the French, and 79 percent of the Japanese said they believed in God, fully 95 percent of Americans said they did. It is noteworthy that in each case a similar percentage said they were willing to die for their country. For the virtues that inspire patriotism—self-discipline, perseverance, industry, respect for family, for learning, and for country—are intimately linked with and strengthened by religious values. In short, the democratic ethic and the work ethic flourish in the context of the Judeo-Christian ethic from which they take their original shape and their continued vitality.

The virtues of self-discipline, love of learning, and respect for family are by no means limited to the Judeo-Christian tradition alone, or to any religious tradition. My point is that in America, our civic virtues are inseparable from our common values. And values such as courage, kindness, honesty, and discipline are common to almost all religious traditions. But it is the Judeo-Christian tradition that has given birth to our free political institutions; and it is the Judeo-Christian tradition that has shaped our national ideals. Although we should never forget the contributions of a host of people from other religions and cultures who have come to our shores in search of freedom and opportunity, we should also acknowledge that freedom and opportunity have flourished here in a political and social context shaped by the Judeo-Christian tradition.

In a book called *The Vietnamese Gulag*, a recent immigrant named Doan Van Toai describes his escape to America after years spent in a Communist prison. Toai marvels at the liberty of our society and at our license to take it for granted. "Perhaps," he tells us, "it is the immigrants' function from generation to generation to remind [Americans] of what a treasure it is they own."

One of the treasures of America is the treasure that Tocqueville called the "civil religion" and that Jefferson called the "general religion." This is the national creed that distills values common to all sects, in all religions, from all cultures. Neither Tocqueville nor Jefferson could have anticipated the variety of faiths that would eventually find a home in America—more than three hundred denominations at last count. Much divides each of these denominations from the others—small questions of doctrine or large questions of revelation. But what is agreed upon is important. It has content and power. It infuses American life with a sense of transcendence. All profit from it, although none is forced to assent to it. And, as the Founders predicted, the constitutional order depends on it.

To protect religious liberty, the Founders sought to outlaw a state religion and to moderate religious passions. At the same time, they recognized that religious values require public acknowledgment, common defense, and mutual respect. And nothing has happened in the past two centuries to suggest that Washington and Madison and John Adams and Jefferson were wrong. All of them envisioned a government neutral between religions in particular but sympathetic to religion in general. For they knew that to be indifferent to the vitality of religious belief is to be indifferent to the vitality of our constitutional order.

NINETEEN

In Defense of
Our Common Language*

OUR ORIGINS are diverse, yet we live together as fellow citizens, in harmony. In America we can say *"E Pluribus Unum"*; out of many, we have become one. We cherish our particularities, and we respect our differences. Each of us is justly proud of his own ethnic heritage, but we share this pride in common, as Americans, as American citizens.

To be a citizen is to share in common principles, common memories, and a common language in which to discuss our common affairs. Our common language is, of course, English. And our common task is to ensure that our non-English-speaking children learn this common language. We entrust this task, in part, to our schools. We expect them, in this as in other respects, to prepare our youth to participate fully in the opportunities and challenges of American society. That is why we become so concerned when we discover that our schools are, in various ways, falling short of what we expect of them. We expect much of them—to impart basic skills, to help form character, to teach citizenship. And we expect our schools to help teach all of our students English, the common language that will enable them to participate fully in our political, economic, and social life.

* This chapter is based on an address delivered to the Association for a Better New York, New York City, September 26, 1985.

Teaching non-English-speaking children English is not a new task for us. It has been performed, with fair success, in communities across this nation since its beginning. But only in the mid-1960s did the federal government accept responsibility for assisting in this task. The timing was no accident. For America was then engaged in a peaceful revolution—our civil rights revolution—in which the federal government stepped in to make good on the great American promise of equal opportunity for all. And this promise extends with full force to those of our children who speak little or no English.

Many of these children are the sons and daughters of immigrants and refugees, who have left behind their homes and all that was familiar to them to come to this land of freedom and opportunity. Many of these children grow up in circumstances that are not easy, their parents struggling day to day for the sake of a brighter future for their children. Other Americans have always, in their churches and communities, done their part to help give such children a chance to achieve that brighter future. It was reasonable and proper, twenty years ago, for the federal government to step in to play a role as well.

How well has our government done by these children? The answer, I am afraid, is not very well. But not from a lack of trying. We began with the best of intentions. We began with two legislative landmarks, the Civil Rights Act of 1964 and the Elementary and Secondary Education Act of 1965. But in both cases, after sound beginnings, federal policies went astray. In a now familiar pattern of events, over the next two decades our policies gradually became confused as to purpose and overbearing as to means. As a result, too many children have failed to become fluent in English, and have therefore failed to enjoy the opportunities they deserve. It is time to get our policies back on track and deliver the equal opportunity so solemnly pledged twenty years ago.

That pledge is nowhere more solemnly expressed than in the 1964 Civil Rights Act:

No person in the United States shall, on the ground of race, color or national origin, be excluded from participation in, be denied the benefits of, or be subjected to discrimination under any program or activity receiving Federal financial assistance.

The federal government set about enforcing this provision against discrimination on the basis of national origin. And there were egregious instances of such discrimination. In some school districts in the Southwest, for example, Mexican-American children had been consigned to classes for the mentally retarded merely because of their limited English ability. In 1970 the Department of Health, Education and Welfare therefore decreed that, where minority children were being excluded from effective participation in school, the school district would be required to "take affirmative steps to rectify the language deficiency in order to open its instructional program to these students." The purpose of such steps was clear—to teach these students English; and schools were free to use whatever means they judged would be effective in the pursuit of this goal.

The propriety of this requirement was upheld by the Supreme Court in 1974 in *Lau* v. *Nichols*, a suit brought by the parents of non-English-speaking Chinese students in San Francisco. The Court found that the failure of the San Francisco school system to provide English-language instruction to these students denied the students a meaningful opportunity to participate in the public educational program. And the Court noted: "No specific remedy is urged upon us. Teaching English to the students of Chinese ancestry . . . is one choice. Giving instructions to this group in Chinese is another. There may be others."

Despite the *Lau* decision's endorsement of flexibility of approach, however, the federal government moved in another direction. In 1975 HEW began to require that educational programs for non-English-speaking students be conducted in large part in the students' native language, as virtually the only approved method of remedying discrimination. These regulations were never formally published, for public notice and comment; indeed when HEW was sued and forced to publish them, in August 1980, they aroused a storm of opposition, and they were withdrawn in February 1981. By that time, however, they had served as the basis of some 500 "compliance agreements" negotiated with school districts across the nation.

Because of their intrusiveness and heavy-handedness, these regulations came close to giving bilingual education a bad name. More important, by the time they were withdrawn in 1981, the evidence was becoming increasingly clear that this educational method imposed from Washington was doing very little to help students learn English.

Why did the government turn down this path? Partly because of a foolish conviction that only Washington meant well and knew best. Local school districts, it was thought, could not be trusted to devise the best means of teaching their students English. But the government made this fateful turn for another reason as well. It had lost sight of the goal of proficient *English* as the key to equal educational opportunity. Instead, the federal government increasingly emphasized bilingual education as a way of enhancing students' knowledge of their native language and culture. Bilingual education was no longer seen so much as a means to ensure that students learned English, or as a transitional method until students learned English; rather, it became an emblem of cultural pride, a means of producing a positive self-image in the student.

Pride in one's heritage is commendable. We in the United States cherish our diversity, and local schools should be free—and more, should be encouraged—to foster the study of the languages and heritages of their students in the courses they offer. But the responsibility of the federal government must be to help ensure that local schools succeed in teaching non-English-speaking students English, so that every American enjoys access to the opportunities of American society.

The history of federal funding for bilingual education tells much the same story. The Elementary and Secondary Education Act of 1965 provided federal aid for the education of children from low-income families; this could include aid to students who needed help learning English. But Congress wished to target special funds for this purpose. In 1968, therefore, Congress passed the Bilingual Education Act, authorizing federal funding of "new and imaginative" programs to meet the special educational needs of poor children who were educationally disadvantaged because of their inability to speak English. The design of such programs was left, in the words of the Senate committee report, "to the discretion and judgments of the local school districts to encourage both varied approaches to the problem and also special solutions for a particular problem of a given school." It was clear that the *problem* was the inability of many poor children to speak English; and the *solution* was funding for a variety of programs to teach those students English. Leaving the exact character of the programs to the discretion of the local school districts was the only reasonable course, given the diversity of situations in the nation's schools and the inconclusiveness of research as to the best methods of teaching English to those who do not speak it at home.

But despite this promising beginning, the Bilingual Education Act evolved into an act whose purposes were less clear and whose programs were more restrictive. When the act was reauthorized in 1974, Congress curbed local control over program design and prescribed education in the students' native language as the sole method local school districts seeking funds could use. Why this change? Not because research had established the superiority of this method to any of the other possible educational methods, methods which placed greater emphasis on instruction in English. For there was no evidence of such superiority. The change came about because the understanding of the purpose of the program changed; it was no longer the straightforward one of making sure that students acquired proficiency in English. This purpose now existed side by side with an emphasis on the importance of "instruction . . . given with appreciation for the cultural heritage of such children."

The Bilingual Education Act was renewed again in 1978. Funding had by then increased twentyfold, but the research findings were sobering. A four-year study of over ten thousand Hispanic students had concluded that many students in federally funded bilingual programs already knew English, and some had simply been assigned there because of their Hispanic surnames; that those students who did need to learn English had shown little improvement; and that most of the programs, despite their label of "transitional bilingual education," did not in fact lead to a transition to English competency. The director of the study told Congress: "There is no compelling evidence . . . that Title VII bilingual education as presently implemented is the most appropriate approach for these students." Nonetheless, Congress made only minor changes in the law.

The Bilingual Education Act was most recently reauthorized in 1984. Congress had before it yet more evidence that the mandated instruction in the students' native language was no more effective than alternative methods of special instruction using English; and in some cases the mandated method was demonstrably less so. Indeed, the English-language skills of students in bilingual education programs seemed to be no better than the skills of those who simply remained in regular classrooms where English was spoken, without *any* special help. In addition, Hispanic children, the largest subgroup of the eligible population, had continued to perform scholastically far below the national average.

The recent news of gains by Hispanic students in SAT scores is welcome indeed and is testimony to the impressive efforts of many Hispanic parents and children. Yet we cannot take these scores as a sign that all is well; the scores of Hispanics remain unacceptably below the national average. More important, these scores reflect the achievement of only *half* of all Hispanic children. Almost half of Hispanic high school students drop out before graduation; and of these dropouts, 40 percent never reach the tenth grade. This figure is as tragically high now as it was twenty years ago.

In response to these facts, and in response to the influx of immigrants from various parts of Asia and elsewhere—for whom many schools find it practically impossible to provide native-language instruction—Congress has recognized the need for programs using alternative instructional methods. These methods include "English as a second language" and "structured immersion" and they provide special instruction *in English* to students of limited English proficiency. Congress did allow, in its 1984 reauthorization, for such alternative programs, but it limited funding for those programs to 4 percent of the total appropriation, leaving local school districts still very much constrained. And Congress unfortunately further backed away from a clear statement of the goal of learning English, by authorizing for the first time funding for programs designed simply to maintain students' competence in their native language.

This, then, is where we stand: After seventeen years of federal involvement, and after $1.7 billion of federal funding, we have no evidence that the children whom we sought to help have benefited. And we have the testimony of an original sponsor of the Bilingual Education Act, Congressman James Scheuer of New York, that the act's "original purposes were perverted and politicized"; that instead of helping Hispanic students learn English, "the English has been sort of thinned out and stretched out and in many cases banished into the mists and all of the courses tended to be taught in Spanish. That was not the original intent of the program."

What, then, is the Department of Education to do? Give up on the promise of equal educational opportunity for those children who are not proficient in English? Our sense of what we owe our fellow Americans will not permit this. Continue down the same failed path on which we have been traveling? This is an equally bankrupt course. We ought to do more for our fellow citizens than throw good money after bad; and we ought to offer more than increasingly hollow protestations of concern and gestures of solidarity.

The Department of Education intends to make good on the promise of equal educational opportunity for all Americans. We shall therefore explore with Congress the possibility of removing the 4 percent cap on alternative instructional methods, as well as other legislative changes; and we shall move, through regulatory and administrative changes, to allow greater flexibility for local school districts. Were Congress to grant the flexibility for local school districts that we seek, I would be prepared to recommend modest increases for funding for these programs. And we shall take care, in the course of ensuring that civil rights are respected, that we do not impose a particular method of instruction.* These reforms will allow local school districts to choose the sort of program or combination of programs best suited to their particular needs. School districts serving recent immigrants who speak seventy different languages obviously need different sorts of programs than school districts whose students speak only two languages.

The Department of Education does not intend to prescribe one method or another. Many school districts will undoubtedly continue to pursue programs with some instruction in the native language; these can be very useful in helping students keep up with their classwork until they become fluent in English. But the goal

---

* In April 1988 President Reagan signed the Augustus F. Hawkins–Robert T. Stafford Elementary and Secondary School Improvement Amendments, by which Congress raised the 4 percent cap on alternative instruction methods to 25 percent.

of any method should be clear: fluency in English. As President Reagan has said, "Bilingual programs should serve as a bridge to full participation in the American mainstream. They should never segregate non-English-speaking students in a way that will make it harder, not easier, for them to succeed in life."

Our movement away from exclusive reliance on one method, and our endorsement of local flexibility, should not be mistaken for a return to the old days of sink-or-swim. Many children in earlier generations learned English in such circumstances; but some did not, and at times the cost was high. We intend to enforce the requirement that school districts provide equal opportunity for students deficient in English by offering programs that address their needs. But we believe that local flexibility will serve those needs far more effectively than intrusive federal regulation. As historian Diane Ravitch points out, "It is unprecedented for the federal government to prescribe a particular pedagogical method. . . . Congress should prescribe the goal—in this case, English-language literacy—and each district should be free to decide how to achieve that goal."

But as this comment suggests, we need also to clarify for ourselves our national commitment to the goal. Paradoxically, we have over the last two decades become less clear about the goal—English language literacy—at the same time as we have become more intrusive as to the method.

There ought to be no confusion over our goal. The rise in ethnic consciousness, the resurgence of cultural pride, in recent decades is a healthy thing; the traditions we bring with us, that our forefathers brought with them to this land, are too worthwhile to be discarded. But a sense of cultural pride cannot come at the price of proficiency in English, our common language.

For one thing, there is overwhelming evidence that English-language proficiency is crucial to social and economic achievement in America. This evidence includes sophisticated econometric studies showing that wage differentials between Hispanics and other Americans, once one takes account of such factors as age and the amount of formal education, are almost entirely accounted for by differences associated with English-language skills. Simply put, the better your English, the more you earn.

The evidence includes the testimony of the leading businessmen who make up the Committee for Economic Development: "We believe," they say in a recent report on American education, "that all Americans must become proficient in the English language in order to work and live in the modern world." And from this they draw the conclusion: "Although this goal should be shared by every school district in the nation, we are aware that the techniques used to accomplish English mastery will need to vary from district to district. Because there is no agreement as to the most effective method for teaching English to non-English-speaking youngsters, such local variation is both necessary and desirable. We support bilingual education as long as English mastery is the end product of the program." And, I would add, so does this administration, and so do the American people.

Mastery of English is the key to individual opportunity in America. And teaching English to those whose native language is not English is a continuation of the struggle to provide for all Americans an equal opportunity to make of themselves what they can. But mastery of English is important for reasons that go beyond individual opportunity, crucial though that is.

We are, after all, one people, fellow citizens. The Civil Rights Act of 1964 was an affirmation of fellow citizenship based on our moral equality, as well as a means to individual opportunity. As fellow citizens, we need a common language, and that language is English. Our common history is written in English. Our common forefathers speak to us, through the ages, in English. This is not contradicted by the fact that it is an enduring glory of this nation to have welcomed with open arms immigrants from other lands, speaking other languages; nor by the fact that it is a feature of our free society that these languages can continue to find a place here. But beneath the wonderful mosaic of cultures here, beyond the remarkable variety of languages, we are one people.

We are one people not by virtue of common blood, or race, or origin. We are one people, above all, because we hold these truths to be self-evident: that all men are created equal, that they are endowed by their Creator with certain unalienable rights, and that therefore just government is by consent of the governed. And government by consent means government by discourse, by debate, by argument. Such a common enterprise requires a common language. We should not be bashful about proclaiming fluency in this language as our educational goal; and we should not be timid in reforming our policies so as to secure it. For with this goal comes the reward of full participation in this remarkable nation of ours—"not merely a nation but a teeming Nation of nations," as Walt Whitman said—but still, at the end of the day, beneath all the differences of politics and color and creed, one nation, one people.

PART
SIX

IN DEFENSE
OF
THE WEST

TWENTY

Why Western Civilization?*

AT HARVARD UNIVERSITY in the fall of 1986, I delivered an address on the condition of higher education in America. I spoke particularly of the moral and intellectual mission of the academy—as claimed by the academy itself—and of my perception that some of our colleges and universities currently fall short of fulfilling that mission. Among other things, I cited the disappearance of a common curriculum in many of the nation's colleges and universities, and the resulting failure of many students to acquire, after four years of college, even a rudimentary knowledge of the civilization of which they are both products and heirs. Our students, I said, "deserve . . . at a minimum, a systematic familiarization with our own Western tradition of learning: with the classical and Jewish-Christian heritage, the facts of American and European history, the political organization of Western societies, the great works of Western art and literature, the major achievements of the scientific disciplines. In short, the basic body of knowledge which universities once took it upon themselves as their obligation to transmit, in the name of liberal education, from ages past to ages present and future."

Following the speech, a student in the audience asked me

* This chapter is based on an address delivered at Smith College, Northampton, Massachusetts, April 16, 1987.

this question, to resounding applause: Why the West? How, in this increasingly complex world, "can you justify an educational core based solely on an understanding of Western civilization?"

This is a challenge that I have heard before. As chairman of the National Endowment for the Humanities, I released a report in 1984 on the humanities in higher education called *To Reclaim a Legacy*. In that report, I made many of the points that I raised again at Harvard: that in many of our colleges the curricula have become diffuse and directionless; that many of our colleges have lost sight of their fundamental role in conveying our common culture; and that young Americans have become increasingly removed from the very taproots of their society. The study received much attention after its release; I think it is fair to say that it received much acclaim. But it has also had its critics. In a symposium in April 1986 at Yale University prompted by *To Reclaim a Legacy*, a panel of professors from some of the nation's leading colleges and universities reached general agreement that the view of Western culture represented by my report was variously sexist, elitist, imperialist, bourgeois, ethnocentric, racist, selfish, and solipsistic.

I would like to return to some of the issues raised at Harvard. In particular, I would like to take up again the question, Why the West? Why do I believe it is important that Americans study, value and, yes, defend Western civilization?

First, we must study the West because it is ours. It is the culture in which we live and in which most of us will continue to live: it is the water, and we are the fish. We live in a society governed by precepts that are products of Western civilization, and that bear witness to its moral development. The institutions that inform our conduct as a people—our schools and universities, our churches and synagogues, our communities and governments and even our notions of friendship and family—acquired their shape through the course of Western history. The ideals and beliefs that bind us as a people—belief in human rights, the dignity of man, the inviolability of conscience—first gained currency at particular times in Western history. To understand our society, our institutions, our ways, and our contemporary controversies, we need to understand our political, social, and intellectual history. We need to know the story of Western civilization, for that is where our institutions and society were made.

To be sure, the East and other cultures have contributed importantly to our institutions and the ideals that we hold in common. In her 1982 Jefferson Lecture, sponsored while I was chairman of the National Endowment for the Humanities, Emily Vermeule showed how even in classical times the forebears of the Western tradition drew upon other cultures around them. In no field is the Western achievement monolithic. The contribution of the Chinese to science and technology, for instance, is impressive: well before the West, the Chinese were using the iron plow, the compass, and the decimal system. These are considerable achievements, and they indicate a civilization worthy of study. Our students should study other cultures, and study them in greater depth than many now do. And to understand another culture requires more than a quick, often patronizing "bus tour of the Third World," as a colleague of mine put it.

When they take other cultures seriously, students recapitulate another propensity of Western civilization, for it has been one of the abiding strengths of the West that it is inquisitive about other cultures and other societies. Today in the United States, we have the strongest academic anthropological cadre in the world. Western civilization is strong in part because it has learned to be open, to study and learn from others. This is good. But in studying other cultures it is best to begin with a thorough knowledge of our own; knowledge of one's own civilization provides a platform from which to view others. In the words of the American philosopher Arthur E. Murphy, "We do not understand the ideals of other cultures better by misunderstanding our own, or adequately enrich an intercultural synthesis by offering to it anything less than the best that we have."

This, then, is the first reason that we must study the West: it is ours. It is where we live—culturally, socially, morally, and legally. It tells us where we have been and suggests possibilities for where we might want to go.

The second reason we must study, value, and defend Western civilization is because it is good. It is not all good. There are certainly great blots on its record. In the story of the West there are injustices—catalogs of sins and errors. Nevertheless, the West has produced the world's most just and effective system of government: the system of representative democracy. In the story of inhumanity and misery that is history, in the totality of its acts, the Western achievement stands high. The story of the West is the most hopeful story. For, as Allan Bloom has written in *The Closing of the American Mind*, "America tells one story: the unbroken ineluctable progress of freedom and equality."

These are not principles shared the world over. Whole nations and whole political systems exist under which they are systematically denied. Indeed, though these principles represent the best of the West, the culmination of the West, there are parts of the West in which they are not respected. The Soviet Union has roots in Western civilization—deeply buried. Yet the government of the Soviet Union is the world's foremost example of a system that flouts the highest ideals achieved in Western thought.

George Orwell once said that at times the first duty of responsible people is the restatement of the obvious. So allow me to emphasize the obvious: not all systems of government are equal. Some forms of government are better than others; some are more just, less oppressive, more open, less resistant to needed reforms. And first among these forms of government is the liberal democracy of the West. The Founders knew this; Lincoln knew it; Martin Luther King, Jr., knew it. Many of our enemies know it. Liberal democracy is at once the world's greatest form of government and among the greatest products of Western thought and effort—painstaking, at times bloody effort.

I was interested to read of a new study ranking the nations of the world according to the quality of life provided their people. Of the countries listed in the top ten, all but one were in the West. The one Eastern nation—Japan—was, like the nine from the West, a democratic republic. From the western face of the Berlin Wall to the westernmost shores of Japan, liberal democracy has been virtually synonymous with and tantamount to improvement in the standard of living and the quality and value of human life. From Poland to El Salvador to the Philippines, what Lord Bryce observed a hundred years ago is even clearer today: "The institutions of the United States . . . are believed to disclose and display the type of institutions towards which, as by a law of fate, the rest of civilized mankind are forced to move, some with swifter, others with slower, but all with unresting feet." And the brightest beacon to that way of life has been the U.S. Constitution, the most imitated political document in the world. In the fifth century B.C., Pericles could say that Athens was the education of Hellas; in our day, it is the West—the United States especially—to which much of the world looks for guidance, hope, and inspiration.

If the Western political order is the best the world has seen, so too is its philosophical tradition. For every person who seeks serious answers to such questions as "What can I know? What should I do? What should I hope for? What is man? What is good?"—indeed to the very question "How should I live?"—there is no better place to look for guidance than the great books and deeds of the Western tradition. Otherwise, we answer these questions in a void, ignorant of the most thoughtful presentations of fundamental alternatives. There is no need to impoverish ourselves in this way. The Western tradition is an unparalleled resource from which all can learn and profit in the way we lead our lives.

Yet, while the questions that the great books pose are fundamental, the answers that they provide are unpredictable. The great books are in fact a great conversation, in which the conclusions are not fixed beforehand. In the tradition of Peter Abelard, our civilization offers a great *sic et non* on the human condition. Consider: On the merits of the religious life, whom do we follow—Aquinas or Voltaire? On the nobility of warfare—Homer or Erasmus? On the worth of sexual fidelity—Tolstoy or James Joyce? On the place of virtue in politics—Aristotle or Machiavelli?

The case for the study of the liberal arts is not, then, a case for ideology; it is a case for philosophy and for thoughtfulness. Those who take such studies seriously live very different lives and come to very different conclusions about particulars. The tenets of Western civilization are not etched in stone; the West is the most self-critical of cultures. Reason is exalted, and reason leads to a look, a second look, and where necessary, readjustment, redefinition, and change.

It is one of the distinguishing features of Western civilization, in fact, that it has engaged in this dialogue, in self-examination and correction, over the centuries. The Western tradition is one of discussion and dissent as much as one of affirmation and agreement, and there is no greater example than America itself. This is a country that declared itself independent from the Old World so that a new political order might be established. That new, American order was one arrived at by reason and examination, calling upon centuries of discussion and debate, and it was one that dissented from an age-old political tradition still embodied in the European states of the time. When it was formed under the Constitution, this new country was designed specifically to accommodate—indeed, to promote—tensions between divergent political beliefs. John Adams called the Constitutional Convention itself "the greatest single effort of national deliberation that the world has ever seen."

In our two hundred years under that Constitution, deliberation has been a central characteristic of our democratic government. It was open deliberation and dissent that helped Abraham Lincoln convince the nation that slavery must be overcome; in this century, it was open criticism and dissent that enabled Martin Luther King finally to topple Jim Crow.

So again, the second reason that we should study, nurture, and defend the West is because it is good. It has not always been good; it is not now all good. But, as Leszek Kolakowski said in his Jefferson Lecture a year ago:

> However distasteful our civilization might be in some of its vulgar aspects, however enfeebled by hedonistic indifference, greed, and the decline of civic virtues, however torn by struggles and teeming with social ills, the most powerful reason for its unconditional defense (and I am ready to emphasize this adjective) is provided by its alternative. It faces a new totalitarian civilization of Sovietism and what is at stake is not only the destiny of one particular cultural form but of humanity as we have known it.

The third reason we must study, value, and defend the West is because the West is under attack. It is under attack from those who declare themselves hostile to Western progress, Western principles and, in some cases, Western religions. This attack comes from without, of course, but also from within. It comes from those so taken in by relativism that they doubt the preferability of civilization to savagery, of democracy to totalitarianism. Theirs is not an America that, despite its imperfections, its weaknesses, its sins, has served as a beacon to the world; instead, theirs is an America corrupt with a host of unholy "isms," such as racism, elitism, and imperialism. So it is, for example, that in the Yale symposium I mentioned earlier, a speaker explained—to ecstatic applause from his colleagues—that diminishing the study of the West is one important step toward freeing the world from "the final fruits of bourgeois humanism: North Atlantic ethnocentrism."

I would like to respond to one in particular of the charges frequently brought against the West: the charge of sexism. In addition to being racist, imperialist, and the like, the West is said by a very vocal—and influential—minority to be characterized by a nearly pathological mistreatment of women. For example, a central feature of the 1985 World Conference on Women in Nairobi was the denunciation of Western education, Western economics, and Western defense.

But I ask: On balance, is there another culture that has been better for women? To be sure, men and women have not been treated equally throughout our past. Yes, grant the injustices of earlier times. Grant the injustices of our day. But grant as well that in America today, women enjoy more liberty, more opportunity than they ever have before. And grant that women in the West are far better off than women anywhere else in the world.

It has been said that the rights of man were the rights of Englishmen first. In a sense this is true: the rights that we consider self-evident today were not always so evident; they were not always acknowledged. They were first expressed by the British, and first secured by Americans. In the same way, it may be said that what we consider today the rights of mankind were first the rights of men; the rights proclaimed two hundred years ago in this country have only in this century been fully accorded to women. But today, they are indeed the rights of both men and women.

As citizens, women enjoy all the privileges and freedoms of democratic citizenship; they enjoy the right to vote, to speak, to worship, and to associate freely. These are privileges enjoyed by neither men nor women under nearly any other form of government. And these were rights achieved, like the abolition of slavery, by appeal to the first principles of liberal democracy: that is, to the best in the tradition of the West. So it was that the Declaration of Sentiments, issued by the first Women's Rights Convention in Seneca Falls, New York, in 1848, harked back to the principles and very language of the Declaration of Independence. Likewise, it was through the process of free deliberation and self-correction provided under the Constitution that, with the ratification of the Nineteenth Amendment in 1920, women finally gained the right to vote.

So, yes, the West may be accused of grave transgressions against women. In the past it has been guilty of many. So has every civilization. What distinguishes the West, however, is not that it has been especially discriminatory, paternalistic, sexist, or any of the other epithets frequently blown about. What distinguishes the West is the opposite. The West stands apart because, unlike other civilizations, it has slowly but steadily removed barriers to women. Women, like men, live as citizens of a free country; women, like men, have the opportunity to make of themselves what they will. And this includes choosing "traditional" roles as well as others.

These freedoms exist in few other societies. In fact, the blessings of life in this country are sought by people of all races and all creeds the world over. They are sought by men and women alike. The everyday conditions of life in the West are but an aspiration, a dream, for most women and men of the world.

Not long ago I came across an article which noted that one prominent feminist had taken to calling conservative women like Margaret Thatcher and Jeane Kirkpatrick "female impersonators." The point, apparently, was that to be a real woman, one must hew to a particular party line. Judging by her choices, an essential element of that party line was opposition to a strong national defense.

This comment reflects the worst sort of sexism, and an ideological chill fundamentally at odds with the openness characteristic of discourse in the West. I consider Margaret Thatcher and Jeane Kirkpatrick to be two of the foremost defenders of the West today. All Americans should be proud to stand with them. And they should be proud to stand with Corazon Aquino in defense of democratic government, and with Coretta Scott King in defense of civil rights. These women are among the most distinguished leaders of our day. And they are distinguished, above all, by their defense of the West.

If it can be said that today there is one objective to which all Americans should adhere, I believe that it is the defense of the

West and the extension of its principles. To those who are most concerned with justice, with equality, with human dignity, there can be no greater cause. The places today where the rights of women are most threatened are the places where the rights of all people are systematically denied, the nations, in short, where the ideas developed over 2,500 years in the West have failed to prevail. For all of us, for women as for men, these ideas, these Western ideas, remain still the last, best hope on earth.

TWENTY-ONE

America. the World.
and Our Schools*

DOES THE TEACHING of international politics have a place in American secondary education, in education for democratic citizenship? I believe that it does. In fact, it always has. To cite a great nineteenth century educator by the name of Abraham Lincoln, every American's schooling should equip him "to read the histories of his own and other countries, by which he may duly appreciate the value of our free institutions."

Even then, Americans were taught the most important lesson of international politics—what their own system of government meant as opposed to most of the systems of government they saw overseas. And, from the first, Americans hoped that their particular experiment in self-rule would ultimately affect the political institutions everywhere in the world.

Some of this hope has been rewarded. But not everyone has followed our lead. Today the continent of Europe is divided between nations in full democratic flower and nations crushed by occupying armies and totalitarian regimes. In such a world there is conflict. We have global responsibilities, and international politics have a more pressing claim on our attention than ever before.

* This chapter is based on an address delivered to the Ethics and Public Policy Center, Washington, D.C., December 5, 1986.

We need to know—and pass on to our children—as much about the world as we possibly can.

Technology has assisted with the task. When a movement for democracy took hold in the Philippines in February 1986, Americans (and American children) saw its leaders interviewed on television—even before their victory had been secured. And our children see summit meetings and Ayatollahs and hostages and Soviet tanks rumbling through Afghanistan.

There is evidence of more formal effort as well. For secondary schools, new social studies curricula are being developed by men and women mindful of the need for an American electorate knowledgeable about foreign policy. In higher education, the subject has come into its own as a distinctive discipline. In 1976, American universities awarded as many Ph.D.s in international studies as they had in the first forty years of this century combined.

But this evidence is deceptive. It may not point toward widespread knowledge. Relatively few Americans will ever earn a Ph.D. in international studies. And I have found that there is no guarantee that those who do will see the world as it truly is, in its fundamental aspects. So how much do *most* American students know about the world we live in? How well do Americans understand the fundamental character of international politics today— that our republican government stands for certain things in the world, and that other regimes stand against us?

Do they understand that the United States represents something more than the interests of a big power in global competition? That our international posture embodies our founding principles? That we stand as a free, self-governing society in defense of those ideas which together make for freedom and self-government? Respect for the individual. Religious freedom. The rule of law. Limited government. Private property. The freely given, uncoerced consent of the governed. Rights to dissent: freedoms of speech, press, association, and assembly. Majority rule. And do they understand that these ideas are not shared universally, throughout the world? That in some places only lip service is paid to them; that they are honored in words, dishonored in practice?

In the present international arrangement, there exists another idea. It is an idea backed by incredible armed strength. It is an aggressive idea that does not shrink from the use of that strength. And it is an idea of nearly illimitable darkness. In the territories to which it has spread, not a single ideal that Americans believe universal and good and beyond dispute still shines. Except, of course, in the hearts of its bravest victims.

The year 1986 was the twenty-fifth anniversary of the Berlin Wall. After all these years, men and women are still willing to risk death to cross over it, from East to West, to breathe the air of freedom. They do not often succeed. For example, a young man recently attempting to escape to the West reached the top of the wall, only to be cut down in a hail of machine gun bullets. Witnesses heard an East German border guard yell, "I got you, you swine," at the young man's corpse. Which led another East German guard, unable to countenance the murder, to shout at his colleagues in disgust. The protesting guard was quickly disarmed and led away, God knows where.

Are we teaching young Americans to understand the Berlin Wall—its history and its significance? When a Communist dictator like Erich Honecker calls the wall an "anti-fascist protective rampart," are students able to hear this doublespeak for what it is? Do they know what "dictatorship of the proletariat" means? Can they grasp the significance of a totalitarian state, which recognizes no inviolable individual rights? Are they familiar with calculated liquidations? With terror as an instrument of state policy? With the NKVD and KGB? With planned famine, purges, show trials, a pact with Hitler, a gulag? Do Americans recall the fate of Cambodia? Are they aware of current developments in Ethiopia? And can they therefore see why free men and women resist the expansion of communism around the world?

If our children are, in the words of Professor Paul Gagnon of the University of Massachusetts, "unarmed for public discourse," it is in most cases not their fault. Blame for this situation falls on all of us whose job it is to educate American children. And responsibility for making good the failure is ours as well.

How do we do it? By emphasizing facts, for one thing. There is now in our secondary schools no shortage of curricula for the teaching of international politics. But in general I'd say they don't pay much attention to facts. Far from it. Sometimes their basic premises are nonfactual. Consider the various "nuclear age" or "peace" curricula. These begin with the assumption that American children are terrified by the prospect of nuclear annihilation. As it happens, there is no reliable evidence for this claim—in fact, students are much more worried about drugs than nuclear war—but to the advocates of such curricula this just proves the depth of children's terror, which, they say, has been completely repressed.

As "therapy," the curricula attempt to bring the fear and horror out in the open. Students are made to watch graphic films of victims from the Hiroshima and Nagasaki bombings. They play games in which they contemplate their own deaths. They draw concentric circles on maps of their own neighborhoods, simulating the geography of destruction a nuclear explosion might create.

Does fear foster prevention? Does panic foster knowledge? Will the vision of apocalyptic war usher in an age of utopian peace? Is this the sort of education in international politics our students deserve? No. It is not the business of American pedagogy to base its curricula on what are imagined to be its students' fears. And it is not the business of American education to encourage unreasoning fear of any kind.

Nor is it proper to use American classrooms for "creating a grassroots network of educator activists," as Educators for Social Responsibility, one of the most aggressive advocates of peace curricula, has described its goal. In an educational system with a limited but difficult mission—to teach basic knowledge, basic skills, and the values necessary for democratic citizenship—there is no place for propaganda or political activism of any sort, on any side. For the most part, peace studies are the creation of a *political* movement that seeks at least a nuclear freeze, at most unilateral disarmament. This movement has designed lesson plans calling for students to petition their elected representatives about the threat of nuclear war. It has urged that our schools institute "infusion workshops" in which teachers set aside entire days "to grow in enthusiasm for justice and peace education." This is not education; this is indoctrination. And much of it is just what it sounds like—a perfectly preserved fossil of 1960s-style political activism.

Another legacy from the Age of Aquarius that has been enshrined in too many of our social studies curricula is a disturbing antirational bias. Curriculum guides for what is known as "global education" are shot through with calls for "raised consciousness," for students and teachers to view themselves "as passengers on a small cosmic spaceship," for classroom activities involving "intuiting," "imaging," or "visioning" a "preferred future." Two proponents of such curricula have offered a candid caution: "These exercises may seem dangerous to your logical thought patterns. For best results, suspend your judging skills and prepare to accept ideas that seem silly and/or impractical." Well, if we're going to give up critical judgment, we'd better give up the game of education altogether.

Then there is the grandest shibboleth of them all—the idea that we must never judge other societies or other political systems. Indeed, the habit of making such judgments is alleged to be a major failing of the old way of teaching about the world. As guidelines published by the National Council for the Social Studies put it, the traditional social studies curriculum "reflected the biases of the white middle class" and distorted non-Western cultures.

But it is this society, after all, in its freedom, its scholarship, and its tolerance, that has established a matchless record for its willingness to provide an open and sympathetic hearing for diverse ideas. It is this country, is it not, that sends open-minded social scientists and cultural anthropologists to study even exceedingly close-minded, ethnocentric societies abroad. We have profited from those studies; we are committed to learning from the customs and the values of other cultures and other societies. And we have a historically unprecedented appetite for self-scrutiny and self-criticism.

Now, I happen to believe that a rational, realistic, and open-minded approach to international politics is possible for American high schools. But we do not have to teach this subject as diluted cultural anthropology, arguing in effect that all the world's governments are the same because all their people drink water and breathe air, and that no society's practices are better than any other's. To put the matter succinctly: you cannot fit liberal democracy and communism together on any map of the world's moral landscape. Wishes will not replace the fact that American citizens share almost nothing of their political life with the subjects of a totalitarian government.

That American textbooks should eschew xenophobia is obvious. They should, clearly and factually, teach our children what they need to know about other countries and their cultures. But openness and honesty require, as well, the acknowledgment that not all systems are humane, decent, or legitimate. This is not ethnocentrism but, to the contrary, an honest commitment to universal criteria of judgment that requires us to discriminate among the societies of the world. All men are created equal; but all political and social systems are not. By universal criteria, some are simply awful: their people live in misery, oppressed by their governments and denied their dignity. Just as we do not shrink from telling the truth about American slavery, let us tell the horrible truth about the extermination of tens of millions in Stalin's Russia. Let us, in short, tell the whole truth.

The central fact of today's political world is the defensive opposition of the United States and its democratic allies to the Soviet Union and its empire. If I urge our schools to communicate this fact to our students, am I urging that they be "indoctrinated"? By no means. Let me emphasize—I do not care whether textbook publishers or teachers approve or disapprove of particular American foreign policies. They're free citizens, it's a free country. They're entitled to their opinions. But as educators, their obligation is to tell the truth.

Americans instinctively abhor governments that attempt to enforce intellectual conformity on their people. But certain things must be told. We cannot abdicate our responsibility to inform our children about the world around them. Too many of our textbooks tell us only that communism is an ideology that preaches common ownership of property and wealth, that Communist nations like the Soviet Union have reduced illiteracy, and that, as one American textbook asserts, "equality for women in the USSR is a reality. . . . They may marry or vote when they are 18." Vote? Vote for what?

So, how should our high school students be taught international politics? What is "global education," properly understood?

Students should learn geography and foreign languages, some foreign literature, and a lot of European history. They should be familiar with Western civilization's religious traditions and with the central place of religion in the lives of its peoples. They should be aware of totalitarianism's contempt for the triumph of religious liberty in the West, and of the unnatural superseding of God by man and state under communism.

Students should learn about the Greeks, and about the Romans; about feudalism, the Magna Carta, the Renaissance, and the Enlightenment; about the French Revolution, the Industrial Revolution, and the Russian Revolution; about World War I and World War II.

Our children should know first about themselves. About American literature and American history. And American democracy. What are its basic elements, its fundamental ideas? The values necessary to sustain it, and the conditions for its success or failure? And then they should know about totalitarian regimes. What are their ideological roots? What social conditions gave rise to them? How do they act toward their own people and toward other nations? Students should know about the social, political, and economic arrangements in today's world differentiating the few islands of the free and democratic and the vast encroaching ocean of the unfree and despotic.

Finally, our high school students should learn about the key events of the last forty years that have made relations between the United States and the Soviet Union what they are. What happened at Yalta? Why was Churchill so agitated? What was the Marshall Plan? What is "containment?" What happened in East Germany and Hungary and Czechoslovakia and Cuba? What is happening in Poland and Afghanistan and Nicaragua today? What was America fighting for in Vietnam?

What do human rights mean? In 1982 the National Council for the Social Studies published a booklet entitled *International Human Rights, Society, and the Schools*. It was designed to help social studies teachers teach about human rights, as they should. But the booklet said there was more than one human rights tradition: "In Western Europe and the United States, civil and political rights such as freedom of speech, voting, and due process are of prime concern." That's right. But "in Eastern European countries, economic rights such as the right to work, to form trade unions, to strike, and to take vacations are considered essential. . . . The rights which are deemed most important depend upon the social, economic, legal, and political traditions of the people." That's wrong. Ask Lane Kirkland about workers' rights in Eastern Europe. Ask Lech Walesa.

This won't do, and not just because Eastern European rights to form unions and to strike are a hallucination. The Soviet constitution grants its citizens a long list of rights; the trouble is they cannot be exercised. But when our children read about the Soviet constitution, they should be struck by more than the difference between paper and reality; every society falls short of its noblest ambitions. But are the ambitions themselves real, or are they hypocritical—are they a lie?

In short, I am suggesting that the best global education for American students is the truth—the truth about ourselves, our political culture, and our intellectual legacy. And the truth about the world, in all its friendly and hostile aspects, for all its good and all its evil. Though our scholars and our statesmen are forever adding to its finer contours, we are, most of us, agreed what the bulk of that truth looks like. It is high time, I think, that we began making sure our children can see it too.

TWENTY-TWO

Education for Democracy*

OVER THE LAST four decades the Western sector of Berlin has been on the front line of freedom. A city under siege, it has been subject to blockade, threats, and harassment. And yet, drawing strength from a courageous and dedicated people. Berlin has refused to bow before totalitarian pressures. Today, the fate of this city is undeniably and inextricably tied to the larger cause and fate of freedom. The entire Western world has a claim in Berlin, where freedom and tyranny stand face to face, and where a people—one people, the German people—are artificially divided.

What divides this city is, of course, the Berlin Wall. The wall has become a universal symbol, an affront not just to Germans but to every believer in liberty; the most visible demonstration of the failures not just of one particular Communist nation, but of the Communist system in general. For as long as the Berlin Wall stands, it will bear this witness to the world: If you seek to know the truth about the differences between democracy and communism, between freedom and tyranny, between West and East, then come here, 110 miles inside the German Democratic Republic, to this city separated by a wall.

I admit to having been troubled in recent years by a tendency

* This chapter is based on an address delivered at the Amerika Haus, West Berlin, July 9, 1987.

among some in the West—on both sides of the Atlantic—to blur the distinctions between democratic and totalitarian governments. These individuals have suspended moral judgment against an intrinsically evil system, a system responsible for the subjugation of the entire eastern half of the European continent. There has arisen a reluctance by some in the West to face up to the harshness of the precepts and practices of totalitarianism: the absolute primacy of the state over the rights of the individual; the unlimited use of coercive state power to transform society, culture, and personality; the systematic attempts to deny individuals their most basic human rights—the right to dissent, the right of self-government, and the freedoms of speech, press, association, assembly, and religion.

At the same time, the West is in danger of losing something solid at the core: faith in the justice and truth of our democratic cause. We have seen over the years troubling signs of indifference to the cause of preserving and defending freedom. There are signs that the West is in danger of suffering an erosion in what the great and prophetic Aleksandr Solzhenitsyn called "civic courage."

There is a good deal of evidence to support these claims. Let me offer just two examples. The first are the results of a poll taken in Western Europe in late 1986. In response to the question "Which country do you believe is making a greater effort to bring about a nuclear arms control agreement, the United States or the Soviet Union?" the responses broke down this way: In Britain, 20 percent said the United States was making a greater effort while 46 percent said the Soviet Union; in France, 35 percent said the United States, while 20 percent said the Soviet Union; and in West Germany, 18 percent said the United States, while 42 percent said the Soviet Union.

In response to the question "Who is more trustworthy, President Reagan or Soviet leader Gorbachev?" 29 percent of those polled in Britain said Reagan was more trustworthy, while 21 percent said Gorbachev. In France, 47 percent said Reagan, while 10 percent said Gorbachev. And in West Germany, 26 percent said Reagan, while 33 percent said Gorbachev. According to this poll, then, more Germans trust Mikhail Gorbachev than trust Ronald Reagan. These data are worth reflection—hard reflection.

Western democracies are not without fault. Our history is not spotless; mistakes have been made. Nevertheless, I find it difficult, even perplexing, to understand the refusal by some to make elementary moral distinctions between those who seek, sometimes imperfectly, to liberate the human spirit against those who seek—in a manner consistent with the dogmas of Marxism-Leninism—to subjugate the human spirit. The words that President Kennedy spoke in Berlin almost a quarter of a century ago still ring true today: "Freedom has many difficulties," he said, "and democracy is not perfect, but we have never had to put a wall up to keep our people in, to prevent them from leaving."

This essential truth should not be lost. There are some very real, and some very tragic, examples we can look to. We need only look to the victims of Soviet tyranny in Budapest and Prague and Kabul. We need only look to Lech Walesa and the people of Poland. We need only look to the people trapped inside the Eastern sector of Berlin.

Yet, even as the brick and mortared symbol of what divides East from West stands in full view, we have witnessed a troubling paradox emerge. While democratic nations of the West have made gigantic strides in the direction of greater freedom and social justice, totalitarian states have produced wars, holocaust, economic misery, concentration camps, and gulags. Yet in spite of this record, the paradox is that faith and belief in the principles of liberal democracy—and in those who would defend liberal democracy—has wavered in the West. In the words of the eminent philosopher and social critic Sidney Hook, "Unless that faith and that belief can be restored and revivified, liberal democracy will perish."

How, then, do we restore and revivify our faith in liberal democracy? A good place to start, the best place to start, is with the education of our young. Many of the intellectual and moral failures we are now experiencing are the logical outcome of not teaching students the differences between democracy and other, less worthy forms of government, of not teaching students *why* they should cherish democratic ideals. Children are not born knowing these things instinctively; a love of democratic principles, and an understanding of why they are so important, must be taught explicitly. They must be taught in the schools of any democracy that wishes to survive. They must be passed from generation to generation.

Two different but persuasive authorities are worth calling on here. One is Richard Lowenthal, former professor of international relations, and now professor emeritus, at the Free University of Berlin. According to Lowenthal, the West faces a "crisis in our civilization" owing to a

> rejection of any time perspective in the name of a cult of immediacy; for the sense of measured time and the gearing of action to foresight have been basic for all Western civilization from the age when Western church-towers were first endowed with clocks to the latest achievements of science and industry. In other words, we are witnessing a major failure to transmit an important part of our basic values to a significant part of the young generation.

The second authority I would like to call on is Thomas Jefferson. Jefferson, in addition to being one of the fathers of our country, was also one of the fathers of our system of education. He knew that an educated, informed citizenry is vital to the well-being of every democracy, because democracies depend on individuals making intelligent decisions, both on election day and in the day-to-day conduct of their affairs. Jefferson therefore knew, for example, how important it is that the citizens of a democracy be literate.

But he also knew that literacy in itself is not enough for the survival of a democracy; it is a necessary but not sufficient condition. In listing what he saw as the fundamental aims of education in his new country, Jefferson, wrote that schools should teach every student

> to understand his duties to his neighbors and country, and to discharge with competence the functions confided to him by either. . . . To know his rights . . . and in general, to observe with intelligence and faithfulness all the social relations under which he shall be placed. To instruct the mass of our citizens in these, their rights, interests and duties, as men and citizens, are . . . the objects of education.

Jefferson, of course, had lived through one revolution, and he knew that liberty is a difficult commodity to obtain. He also knew that, once acquired, it is just as difficult to preserve freedom; the task requires, as he put it, the "diligence, candor, and judgment" of each new generation. As Goethe observed, "You must labor to possess what you have inherited." It is, then, the unique responsibility of educators in a democracy to teach democratic principles to their students.

What are the essential assumptions and values of democratic civilization that our schools must teach? I begin with certain political principles to which all democrats would subscribe. These principles travel under different names from time to time—natural rights, individual rights, human rights—but Jefferson called them "unalienable rights," and I don't think anyone has ever improved on that phrase. We believe in liberty, and we believe in equality. We believe in the freely given, uncoerced consent of the governed. We believe that all men and women are entitled to political equality without discrimination based on race, sex, or creed. We cherish certain rights such as freedom of speech, freedom of the press, freedom of assembly, and freedom of religion. And we believe that government should be limited in its powers, and that government's essential purpose is to protect these unalienable rights of its citizens. These are things in which the citizens of all democracies believe, and our children should be taught them in our schools.

Democracies are also built upon respect for certain institutions. We believe in the crucial importance of representative government based on free, competitive elections. We believe in an independent judiciary upholding the rule of law. We affirm the centrality of the family, the first and foremost agent in the rearing of children. We affirm the importance of church and synagogue. And in all our institutional arrangements, we seek to maximize individual freedom and choice.

Its institutional arrangements and political principles are not the whole of the democratic way of life. There are also certain beliefs about ourselves and our universe in which democratic societies have put their faith. These include belief in the preeminence of reason; in the spiritual nature of man; in learning, scholarship, and free inquiry; in the proposition that the human condition can be bettered; and in the moral imperative to better it.

And finally, the preservation of democracy depends on schools helping to instill certain traits of character. Jefferson wrote that schools must improve students' "morals and faculties" because he understood, as the ancient Greeks understood, that the entire community ultimately depends on the character of its individual citizens. And Jefferson understood that the democratic way of life is possible only when individual citizens possess a certain kind of character. That character must be shaped, above all, by the family. But teachers must help, by the examples they set and by the habits they teach—habits like self-discipline and hard work. They must teach respect for the law, willingness both to offer and accept criticism, and the value of individualism. They must show students the difference between honesty and dishonesty, ambition and greed, loyalty and servitude, liberty and license. And they must teach students not only to recognize what is best and right among these things but to love what is best and right among them. For the theory of democracy can always exist in the statement of these attributes, but the *life* of a democracy exists only when its citizens cherish these things and will not let them go.

These, then, are some of the principles, beliefs, and values that schools must teach if democracies are to survive. Some people—and these people will often claim for themselves qualities of open-mindedness, tolerance, and critical thinking—will argue that to teach these things is to indoctrinate. They will argue that the notion of democracy itself implies the absence of a set of prescribed ends in the education of free men and women. And they will argue that if citizens are really to be free to make their own choices, they must not be told to endorse one set of values or one system of government over others—for this is merely indoctrination, and indoctrination violates the tenets of democracy itself.

Refusing to make meaningful distinctions between antithetical value systems or political systems is intellectually vacuous. Yes, democracy as a political theory gives people the greatest possible freedom in choosing how they will conduct their affairs. But democracy is not a doctrine of moral relativism. There is nothing in the political theory of democracy that rules out the assertion that some forms of human behavior are more worthy than others. And there is nothing in the political theory of democracy that rules out the assertion that some systems of government are better than others. Otherwise, a devotion to democracy as a form of government would be self-contradictory. The truth is that democratic government is morally superior to totalitarian government.

Our students should be taught this truth; they should be taught to appreciate this truth; and then, perhaps, they will learn to cherish this truth. And I would add that there is a great deal of difference between teaching children the truth and indoctrinating them.

Not long ago I went out to San Jose, California, to teach an eleventh-grade class. We were talking about the writings of James Madison, and we were discussing what it means when we say that in a democracy, unlike other kinds of government, liberty is the fundamental political principle. A young girl, sixteen or seventeen years old, raised her hand and asked, "Mr. Bennett, do you think the United States is really a better place to live than the Soviet Union?"

I said, "Yes, it is."

"Well," she said, "I'd like to know why you think so—but maybe I shouldn't ask you because you're from the government, so you probably can't tell me the truth."

I asked, "Why don't you think I can tell the truth? Who told you this about your government? Who told you this about the people whom you elected and who are working for you?"

Well, we talked for a few minutes, and in the end I said, "Look, there are a lot of things you should study, a lot of things you should read." And I mentioned some books on United States history and Soviet history, on our government and on their government. Then I said, "But try this test for a society. It's what I call the gates test. If a society has gates, and you raise the gates, which way do the people run? Do they run out, or do they run in? And I think you know that when the Soviet Union raises its gates even a little bit—when the Soviet Union raises its Iron Curtain—people stampede to get out. And every time we raise our gates, people rush to come in. And even when our gates aren't raised, people stand outside and wait as long as it takes to get in." The young lady promised me she would look into these matters.

The Czech novelist Milan Kundera writes in *The Book of Laughter and Forgetting* that "the struggle of man against power is the struggle of memory against forgetting." The Berlin Wall makes forgetting a difficult task. The Berlin Wall reminds us of what totalitarianism—stripped of its doublespeak and public relations ploys—is really all about. It *is* an evil system.

The Berlin Wall should also remind us that the threat to our freedom is very real and that we are engaged in a struggle with an adversary that is backed by incredible armed strength, an adversary that does not shrink from using that strength. Democracies are fragile and perishable institutions. There is no immutable law of history that guarantees their survival. John Stuart Mill, one of the greatest modern exponents of liberty, wrote, "It is a piece of idle sentimentality that truth, merely as truth, has any inherent power denied to error, of prevailing against the dungeon and the stake."

In the defense of democracy, truth is not enough. The citizens of democracies must also be willing to support the arsenals of democracy. We must be willing to maintain our defenses in a manner consistent with the threat posed against us. In the end, our survival and the survival of all we believe in and care most about—the defense of Western civilization and the protection and nurture of our children—will depend on whether we are vigilant and strong and committed in purpose.

When I return to the United States, the message I will take to my countrymen is this: If you ever begin to believe that the cost of maintaining freedom is too high; if you ever begin to believe that democracies may no longer be worth preserving, and protecting and defending; if you ever begin to lose sight of what makes totalitarianism unique, and uniquely evil, then go to Berlin, go to the wall that divides Berlin, and look east. Peer into the long, dark night that has descended upon the eastern half of this city. And remind yourself that what separates our world from theirs—what separates the sun and the shadow—is freedom alone. It is to that cause, our common hope, that we must dedicate ourselves anew.

PART
SEVEN

THE
REAGAN YEARS
AND
BEYOND

TWENTY-THREE

Prospects for Education Reform*

In the *Odyssey*, among the various episodes that divert Odysseus and his crew from their course is a brief sojourn in the land of the Lotus Eaters. Homer tells us that when Odysseus spotted the island, he sent three men ashore to discover who lived there. The messengers, Homer writes, "fell in with the Lotus Eaters, who showed no will to do us harm." The native offered them a taste of the lotus, and once they had eaten it the unsuspecting crew lost all desire to complete their journey. Tennyson wrote a poem called "The Lotus Eaters" which depicts at length how sloth, cowardice, and gluttony creep over the crew and keep them from their journey. Fortunately, Odysseus is able to set things straight by tying the stricken men to the deck, setting the rest to work, and reminding them all of their hopes, their mission, and their ultimate destination.

Recently, I have become worried that our national movement for educational excellence has entered a phase akin to what befell Odysseus' crew in the land of the Lotus Eaters. Increasingly, it strikes me that in some places—in too many places—the education reform movement is being detained, that the journey is in danger of not being completed. I am worried that in some states and in some districts the steering has gone awry long before we have

* This chapter is based on an address delivered to the Education Writers Association, San Francisco, California, April 5, 1987.

reached the destination. And I am concerned that in some places the education reform movement is being hijacked and held for ransom by those who do not have educational improvement as their first priority. We cannot allow this to happen.

Given the consensus of public opinion and solid research, the most striking feature of education reform today is the relative lack of progress—the relative lack of results—before us. By and large, we know what to do; by and large, we agree on what must be done; but by and large, we have not done it. SAT scores are still far below what they were 20 years ago. American students still lag sadly in international comparisons in math and science. American knowledge of geography is poor. We know what to do; there is broad agreement to do it; but we are not yet getting it done.

Let me be clear about what I mean by education reform. *Fundamentally, education reform is a matter of improved results.* It aims directly at bringing about measurable improvements in the knowledge and skills of American students. Education reform looks first to output, not input. This represents a sea change from the overwhelming emphasis on inputs, resources, and processes of the nearly two decades prior to *A Nation At Risk*.

A Nation at Risk, the closest thing we have to a national education grievance list, cited, among other problems, poor performances by American students on a variety of international education tests; a decline in scores on most standardized tests; and a decline in student knowledge in crucial subjects, such as English and physics. It is these things that we must aim to change. Whatever changes we make in American education—and changes clearly are in order—their value must be determined, finally, by their impact on student performance, on what students learn. Improved results—better outcomes—is what we are after: not intentions alone; not action in and of itself; not inputs; but outcomes, results.

In the national campaign to improve results, we have seen some progress. We have taken some important first steps. For one thing, lest anyone say money is lacking, the American people have made resources available. Indeed, the American people have been remarkably generous in their contributions to our schools: in 1987, national expenditures for education will, in real dollars, reach a new high—over $300 billion.

Second, we have achieved a broad consensus on many ideas:

content, character, and choice among them. As we enter a new school year, there is ample new evidence of that consensus. Read the 1987 Gallup Poll of the Public's Attitudes Toward the Public Schools. Take it to heart. In it you will find overwhelming public support for increased parental choice; for greater accountability; for higher and more rigorous academic standards; for schools' role in the formation of character; and for emphasis on the basic subjects of math, English, history, and science. The American people's views are clear, and, significantly, they find broad support in our best research.

Emphasizing results brings with it some other important shifts in our thinking about education. First, emphasizing results means emphasizing achievement. It means emphasizing the achievement of students—holding high expectations and setting correspondingly high standards. Reform also means emphasizing the achievement of teachers and principals. How well do they know their subjects? How well do they teach? How well do they manage their schools? Teachers and principals should be hired ∈n the basis of what they know and can do, not what courses they have taken. They should be paid and promoted according to their performance, not according to the number of additional courses taken in education theory. Pay based on performance is a genuine, original, and indispensable article of education reform; it is endorsed in *A Nation At Risk;* it is suggested in *Time for Results*, the report of the National Governors' Association; and it has the support of the American people.

Second, emphasizing results means emphasizing assessment. In order for states, districts, and individual schools to make the adjustments necessary to improving student performance, they must have timely, accurate information on performance in particular subjects and skills. How are students performing in math in this district? How are students performing in writing in this school? Has achievement gone up or down over the past three, five, and seven years? This is the sort of information necessary to launching effective efforts to improve educational results. Right now, the Department of Education is working to provide more accurate assessments through the National Assessment of Educational Progress. Improving assessment is a task to be undertaken by individual schools, districts, and states as well.

Finally, emphasizing results means emphasizing accountability, not bureaucracy. Another memorable adventure in the *Odyssey* is Menelaus's wrestling match with the sea-god Proteus. While Menelaus struggles to pin him down, Proteus attempts to slip away by assuming different shapes and forms. The education bureaucracy, with its myriad levels and divisions, can have a similarly slippery quality. If we are going to produce results, we must hold individual leaders and institutions accountable for their performance.

Right now, we don't have enough of it. Accountability is the linchpin, the keystone, the *sine qua non* of the reform movement. In our discussions of education in the coming years, at the local, state, and national levels, accountability should be at the top of the agenda.

Of American education as it currently operates, we can say this: in general, if you do a good job educating a group of students, nothing happens to you or for you. Similarly, if you do a bad job educating a group of students, again, nothing happens to you or for you—except, in the latter case, you often will get more money. There are greater, more certain, and more immediate penalties in this country for serving up a single rotten hamburger in a restaurant than for repeatedly furnishing a thousand schoolchildren with a rotten education. This must change.

Schools that produce good results should be rewarded; those that do not should face penalties that will spur them to improve. One way to increase accountability is through state-supported incentives; another is by enabling parents to choose which school their children attend. Both are policies endorsed by the governors report in *Time for Results*.

Achievement, assessment, and accountability, all adding up to results—these are the fundamental principles of education reform. And these are the principles that, in several places, are under assault.

In four years of the movement for education reform, we have grown accustomed to taking a step back for every two steps forward. This is not necessarily bad. Sometimes a mid-course correction is needed to maintain progress toward the ultimate goal. Yet we must be sure that we do not slip to taking two steps back for every one step forward. In my first address as Secretary of Educa-

tion, I said that it would take constant vigilance to sustain education reform. The fact is that political movements, like ships, can
be blown off course. Crews can tire. Crews can lose will.

Finally, crews can mistake their own contentment and security for the final destination. Let there be no mistake: since the
release of *A Nation At Risk*—indeed since before *A Nation At Risk*—
there has been entrenched and determined opposition to education reform. This opposition has taken many forms. Early on, it
was a voice counseling that things are not as bad as they seem.
This was denial. It emerged later as a voice saying that things may
be bad, but they cannot be fixed through the schools. This was
"let's blame society." More recently, it has been a voice saying, "We
really don't know how to make schools work, what needs to be
done." This is undue pessimism.

Perhaps most persistently, opposition to education reform has
surfaced as a voice advising that things might be fixed, they could
be fixed, even that they should be fixed, but they will require lots
of money first. This is polite extortion. This most durable and per-
sistent lament is nothing short of hijacking education reform and
holding it for ransom. The American people have paid and paid
dearly for education, but as yet they have not been given their
money's worth. They have not been given the good results they
and their children deserve.

How do we restore momentum and direction to the education
reform movement? I do not claim to be Odysseus, and I will refrain from recommending lashing anyone to the deck. But let me
emphasize this: in order for education reform to continue, concerned governors, legislators, parents, and educators must not
succumb to sloth. The education establishment possesses its own
remarkable inertia; we cannot afford to add our sloth to it. Those
concerned for education reform must be diligent. They must not
be cowardly in pursuing and defending the reforms most essential
to improving American education: they must push harder than
the force that pushes against them. In order to succeed, they must
beware the gluttony of interested parties, even friendly-seeming
inhabitants of the world of education. Finally, like Odysseus'
crew, we must keep our sights on the destination we are after:
results—achievement, assessment, and accountability.

I believe that we now stand at a critical juncture in the

movement for education reform. We must either go forward with the goals that I have mentioned, or fall back to reliance on inputs, processes, and bureaucracy. This will mean the bureaucratization of reform, which will be the slow death of reform. The outcome is still in doubt. Education reform is neither irredeemably lost nor irreversibly won.

The American people have invested tremendous amounts of hope, trust, and money in education reform. Their investment must not be betrayed. Let's not let anybody or any special interest hijack it. As Odysseus of old might have said, let's bring it home, at last.

TWENTY-FOUR

The Future of
American Conservatism[*]

AMERICAN CONSERVATISM now sets the terms of our national debate. It does so because, without in the least abandoning its principles, it has succeeded in identifying itself with the quintessential American appetite for new challenges and new opportunities. Under the leadership of Ronald Reagan, American conservatism has shed its skin of distrust and defensiveness toward the world in which we live. It has overcome what once was a suspicion, even a dread, of the future. It has become vigorous, bold, assertive—in a word, fully Americanized. While contemporary liberalism has moved away from—in some cases, even against—the mainstream of American political life, today's conservatism is at home with the common sense and the common beliefs of the American people. As a result, where once conservatives resisted the future, they now view it as something to shape. And there is a good chance to do just that.

Consider the sea changes in two areas in which President Reagan has brought about fundamental shifts in national policy: economics and foreign policy. In economics, a historic tax reform was made possible because the underlying terms of economic debate have been transformed. The 97 to 3 vote in the Senate to

---

* This chapter is based on an address delivered to the Heritage Foundation, Washington, D.C., July 8, 1986.

simplify the tax code and to cut top marginal rates nearly in half was a vote of epochal importance. It signified the utter eclipse of the old economics, mistrustful as it too often was of private enterprise, overly trustful as it too often was of government planning. A new understanding has set in of some old truths concerning the entrepreneurial sources of economic growth and well-being, and the role of government as a reliable and steady economic umpire. The practical reforms that have been achieved in the past seven years—the practical successes we have had—rest on a true intellectual revolution. And just as the failed ideas of the past underlay the spirit of malaise which President Carter apparently thought to be our national condition, so this intellectual revolution justifies the optimism with which we face our future.

Foreign and defense policy is the other main arena in which the Reagan revolution has, of necessity, focused its energies. And here too, I believe, we have succeeded in fundamentally overturning the self-indulgent pessimism of the 1970s. In fact, if the President had achieved little else, he would have secured forever his place in American history for his undeviating commitment to the rebuilding of our nation's defenses—the absolute precondition to conducting a sound foreign policy of any kind. And then there were the successes in Grenada and El Salvador, the historic opportunity represented by the Strategic Defense Initiative, and the new realism concerning the threat of Communist expansion, not least in Central America. In light of such tangible achievements as these, it seems fair to say that we have turned a corner. To put it simply: the United States as a nation is becoming a stronger force in the world arena. And, what is more significant, we understand once again why it is important to be strong. Once again we acknowledge the necessity of acting energetically to defend our interests and our values in a dangerous world. For, no less than in the economic sphere, the great success of the Reagan revolution in foreign and defense policy reflects not just particular changes in discrete policies, but rather a transformation in our underlying sense of what America is and what it can accomplish. On this front as well, American conservatism under the leadership of President Reagan has created grounds for optimism about the future.

More remains to be done, of course; the Reagan revolution is not complete. But conservatives do not expect completion or perfection in the things of this world. Just as, when in the wilderness, conservatives knew that there were no lost causes, so they know, while governing, that there are no causes finally and irrevocably won. It will be the task of future Presidents to sustain and enhance and extend what this administration has done to secure our economic well-being and our national security. But that the accomplishments are real and that we are now on the right path—this much is clear.

It is worth pondering for a moment what a peculiar revolution the Reagan revolution has been. True, we seem to have broken with the past, or at least the immediate past. And true, we look forward with fresh expectations to a future of our own shaping. But this has been a revolution presided over and executed by conservatives—which means that it has been accomplished not by abandoning but, to the contrary, by recovering and conserving fundamental institutions, fundamental principles, and fundamental truths. Indeed, it is precisely by reinvigorating our commitment to these principles and institutions and truths that the President has fostered in Americans in general, and in American conservatives in particular, their new sense of optimism and confidence.

So, too, it must be in the areas that still need to be addressed if we are to complete the Reagan revolution. National wealth and military strength are necessary means to national greatness, but they are not, of course, sufficient. As the President has observed, "A nation's greatness is measured not just by its gross national product or military power, but by the strength of its devotion to the principles and values that bind its people and define their character." In the end, national greatness depends on, is embodied in, the character of our people. This in turn depends on, first, our sense of who we are as a nation and what we believe in; second, on the well-being of the institutions we create to express those beliefs; and third, on the values according to which we shape the next generation of Americans. And it is here, in the somewhat amorphous but nonetheless palpable realm of beliefs and attitudes and values, that an effort of national recovery must be mounted if we are to realize our potential as a people.

Now, on this front—on this moral and cultural front—there are also grounds for hope. In fact, it may be that nothing the President has done is more important than his achievement here.

In his evocation of our national memory and symbols of pride, in his summoning us to our national purpose, he has performed *the* crucial task of political leadership. Moreover, he has done this precisely when many were wondering whether such presidential leadership was still possible. If, as the President has said, "in recent years America's values almost seemed in exile," no public act has been more significant than his welcoming them home. The American people have renewed their commitment to our common principles; the task of cultural reformation and reconstruction has begun.

But the task has only just begun; the triumph is nowhere near complete. Far too many decent Americans remain, in effect, on the moral defensive before their own social and cultural institutions. Can Americans be confident that their children are going to inherit the habits and values they themselves honor? Are we confident our children will learn enough about our history and our heritage? Are we confident they will be raised in an environment that properly nurtures their moral and intellectual qualities? Can we be confident in the cultural signals our children receive from our educational institutions, from the media, from the world of the arts, even from our churches? Are we confident that our society is transmitting to our young the right messages—teaching them the right lessons—about the family, about drug use, about respect for religious beliefs, about our meaning as a nation and our responsibilities as individuals? Is the public air conducive to moral and intellectual health, or do we have cause for worry as we contemplate the future well-being of our families, of our children, of our fellow citizens?

This is a very large topic, and I cannot do it full justice here. I am confident—I am certain—that the vast majority of parents have only the best, the soundest, the most sensible hopes for their children. And most do their best to make those hopes a reality. But as a society, we some time ago lost confidence in our right and our duty to affirm publicly what most of us believe privately. It is this confidence we must regain. We allowed the public square to become, in Richard John Neuhaus's term, "naked"; we allowed our social and cultural institutions to drift away from their moorings; we ceased being clear about the standards which we hold and the principles by which we judge. Or, even if we were clear in our own minds, we somehow abandoned public discussion to the forces of moral and intellectual relativism.

As a result, we may be doing our best individually, but as a society we have much to worry about when we consider the context, the environment, the public ethos in which we raise our children. And we are right to worry, because we are in this together. As we learn in Plato's *Gorgias,* no man is a citizen alone. Individuals and families need support; their values need nourishment in the common culture, in the public arena.

On·fundamental issues of individual character and responsibility, on the role of social institutions like religion and the family, on the common purposes of our national life, we have come a long way in the last few years. But this is the work of more than a few years to reinvigorate and restore our common culture. This work is not primarily the business of government. But it is work that those of us in government must be attentive to and supportive of, and to which we can contribute in careful but limited ways. And it is work of supreme importance. Jimmy Carter ran for President promising a government as good as the American people. Ronald Reagan has given us a government worthy of the American people's respect and trust. But are our social and cultural institutions worthy of the American people? Do they promote the qualities and habits and values that we would wish? If they do not, we need to see to it that they are reformed. This task requires appropriate government policies, but it goes beyond government; it represents the completion of the reforms that have already been undertaken.

Let me give three brief examples of the failure of our institutions to fulfill our hopes as individuals, as parents, as citizens. Our children need to learn about our nation—about our history, our heroes, our heritage, our national memories. They need to learn this not simply in order to have pride in our nation but because, as Leszek Kolakowski put it in his Jefferson Lecture, to "learn history" is "to know who we are"; it is to learn "why, and for what [we are] responsible"; it is to learn how this responsibility is to be taken up.

But do our youngsters know what they should know? Is our history a living tradition, a "mystic chord of memory," for us today as it was for our forefathers? We spend far more on education than ever before. We are exposed, through the communications media, to a heretofore unimaginable variety of messages and information. We enjoy cultural opportunities beyond the dreams of generations past. But are we confident that the principles of the Founders, the traditions embodied in our institutions, the memories of our sacrifices, the examples of our statesmen, will be alive in the next generation's minds and hearts? I do not think we can be as confident as we should be.

What is to be done? Government has a role here—especially state and local authorities, which oversee our public schools; and the federal government has an important educational part to play as well—through speeches, reports, recommendations, through the dissemination of ideas and the setting of a national agenda, through funding for various enterprises. Individuals have an even more central role—at home, and in voluntary associations. But above all, we as a society, as a common culture, have to respond to the call of our national history, and to the responsibility it imposes upon us of instilling in our children an informed appreciation of American principles and American practices. The variety of ways in which this can be done will become clearer once we cut through all the pseudo-sophisticated claims and counterclaims, all the educational cacophony and cultural confusion, and decide: yes, we need to know our national experience, so as to know our national purpose.

A second example: the family. This is our most important social institution. And it is perfectly clear that its decline has been disastrous for many of our youth. As individuals, most of us believe in the family. We want strong families; we presumably want government policies that help families; we want our educational and other cultural institutions to support the family; and we try to foster habits and practices that strengthen the family. Yet, as a society, we are distracted by so many currents and cross-currents that, while we earnestly try to help our young people, we tend to lose sight of this basic fact: without strong families, many of our other efforts will be in vain.

There are no simple answers to the question of how to strengthen the family. But as a starting point, there must come the simple, unapologetic public affirmation that the family is an absolute value, and that heroic measures are justified in preserving and strengthening it. As a polity, as a society, as a culture, we now send mixed signals about this—and we get mixed results. In the rates of youth drug use and crime and lesser forms of irresponsibility and waste of talents and opportunities, we see the human cost of those mixed signals. It is a cost we should resolve to bear no longer.

A third and final example: drugs. The Department of Education will release *Schools Without Drugs* in September 1986, and we are introducing many other initiatives that will help parents and school personnel to get drugs out of our schools. Here, once again, government has a definite role to play and individuals and families have an even greater role. But, with the recent deaths of young athletes in mind, let me also ask this: What of the role of our cultural institutions? Our colleges and universities often call society to task for failing to live up to its stated ideals. They set themselves the role of moral gadfly, moral conscience. But what of them? Surely when parents send their children to college, they have a right to expect the college to take some measures to protect their sons and daughters from drugs.

I made this simple point to the Association of Governing Boards of Universities and Colleges in March 1986—the point that colleges and universities had a basic responsibility to care for both the moral and physical well-being of their charges. I said that colleges must protect students from certain influences—drugs, criminals, fraud, exploitation. "Specifically," I said, "parents should be able to expect colleges to do their best to keep pushers off campus, and get drug users and cheats, frauds and exploiters off campus, if they are already there. Parents expect colleges to be positively and publicly and actively against these things. Parents do not expect colleges to be neutral as between decent morality and decadence." And for saying this, I was criticized for sounding like "a small-town PTA president" and for being "simplistic." Well, if our academic and cultural institutions have become so "sophisticated" that they have forgotten their elementary duties and responsibilities, then it is time for us to call them back to first principles and responsibilities.

Every college president should write to his or her students this summer and tell them: "Welcome back for your studies in September, but no drugs on campus. None. Period. This policy will be enforced—by deans and administrators and advisers and faculty—strictly but fairly." Such a policy could in fact be enforced. It should be enforced. And no parent or taxpayer would object if such a policy was announced and carried out. It would be good for our youth, good for our society, and good for our institutions of higher learning. But putting in place such a straightforward policy would require a reinvigoration of our institutions, a resumption of their basic responsibilities.

Such a reinvigoration of our institutions and resumption of responsibilities have, I believe, begun in America. The meaning of the Reagan revolution extends beyond tax reform and a stronger defense to a recovery of our national purpose, a strengthening of our social bonds, a reaffirmation of our common cultural beliefs. This is a task that goes beyond politics, let alone the politics of one administration. But it cannot be accomplished without support from the polity. To borrow a phrase from an earlier era to which the President is fond of alluding, completing the Reagan revolution means embarking upon a national recovery act. It means fashioning, in traditional but also in novel and imaginative ways, support for the social and cultural and, yes, the moral fabric that, in the end, makes possible true greatness, in nations no less than in individuals. In this effort of national recovery, today's generation of Americans, joining a conservative preference for the tried and true to a willingness to embrace the innovative and the bold, face their own rendezvous with destiny.

Index